Mindful Pregnancy for New Moms

The Ultimate Guide for The First Year, What to Expect for Each Trimester, Hypnobirthing, Childbirth, Breastfeeding, And the Secrets No One Tells You

Catherine Taylor

© Copyright 2019 - All rights reserved.

The content contained within this book may not be reproduced, duplicated or transmitted without direct written permission from the author or the publisher.

Under no circumstances will any blame or legal responsibility be held against the publisher, or author, for any damages, reparation, or monetary loss due to the information contained within this book. Either directly or indirectly.

Legal Notice:
This book is copyright protected. This book is only for personal use. You cannot amend, distribute, sell, use, quote or paraphrase any part, or the content within this book, without the consent of the author or publisher.

Disclaimer Notice:

Please note the information contained within this document is for educational and entertainment purposes only. All effort has been executed to present accurate, up to date, and reliable, complete information. No warranties of any kind are declared or implied. Readers acknowledge that the author is not engaging in the rendering of legal, financial, medical or professional advice. The content within this book has been derived from various sources. Please consult a licensed professional before attempting any techniques outlined in this book.

By reading this document, the reader agrees that under no circumstances is the author responsible for any losses, direct or indirect, which are incurred as a result of the use of information contained within this document, including, but not limited to, — errors, omissions, or inaccuracies.

Contents

Chapter 1:
Things I Wish I Knew While Pregnant -------------------------------------- 1

Chapter 2:
Get Your Pregnancy Off to A Good Start ---------------------------------- 7

Chapter 3:
Morning Sickness No More -- 18

Chapter 4:
Nutrition and Food (Must Know Secrets) --------------------------------- 24

Chapter 5:
Approved Exercises -- 44

Chapter 6:
Money Saving Hacks for Maternity Clothing ----------------------------- 52

Chapter 7:
First Trimester Essential Secrets --------------------------------------- 58

Chapter 8:
Second Trimester Essential Secrets ------------------------------------- 67

Chapter 9:
Third Trimester Essential Secrets --------------------------------------- 83

Chapter 10:
Prevent Stretch Marks Hacks -- 94

Chapter 11:
Necessity Bag Items to Bring for Labor -------------------------------- 100

Chapter 12:
Essential Recovery Secrets After Birth -------------------------------- 110

Chapter 13:
Losing the Weight After Birth --- 117

Chapter 14:
Newborn Must Haves --- 126

Chapter 15:
Don't Fall for These Money Traps -------------------------------------- 135

MINDFUL PREGNANCY

FOR NEW MOMS

The Ultimate Guide for The First Year, What to Expect for Each Trimester, Hypnobirthing, Childbirth, Breastfeeding, And the Secrets No One Tells You

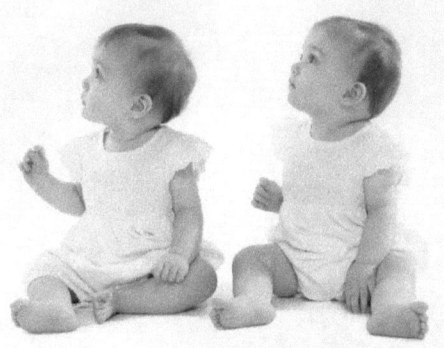

CATHERINE TAYLOR

Chapter 1:
Things I Wish I Knew While Pregnant

The journey of pregnancy is fun, exciting, stressful, and joyful. There's so much to learn during these nine months, and while the journey is something you will always fondly remember, there are going to be times when you wish somebody told you what you were going to experience during these nine months and how you'll feel.

There were so many things I wish I knew during my first pregnancy, so I decided to share this information with you to make your life a little easier. These nine months mark the beginning of a new chapter in your life and the more prepared you are, the better you'll be able to handle it.

Don't Stress About Your Marriage

A lot of pregnant friends tell me they are worried about pregnancy because of the distance they must maintain from their husbands or partners for the first three months. You are most likely going to lose interest in sex during your first trimester, and most women fear their partners may not take it too well.

Honestly, men are just as excited to become fathers, and they are ready to make sacrifices for the well-being of their baby. You'll be surprised how helpful and intimate your partner gets, even though there is no sex during the first trimester. If you're worried about things changing once the baby arrives, don't! I watched my husband transform from a childish boy to a responsible man the minute he held my baby in the delivery room.

If a man truly loves you, he will stick by you through thick and thin, and pregnancy is one of the most cherished moments in a relationship which he is going to enjoy just as much as you do.

Don't shy away from sharing facts about your pregnancy with your husband or partner, make them a part of it and you'll enjoy the journey as a couple.

You Will Get A Chance to Relax!

Ok, I'm going to be honest with you, this might not be exactly post-delivery or for a few months after, but soon enough your baby is going to sleep for long hours, and you're going to rest. A lot of women stress because they say they won't be able to keep up with the feeding demands of a baby. Trust me—once the maternal instincts kick in, all you'll care about is for your baby to have a full tummy and be well rested. The first few months may be stressful, but they are the most beautiful months of your life and watching your little baby grow, is something you will look forward to! Each time you place your baby on the weighing scale, and you see an increase in weight you'll have a proud smile on your face.

Educate Yourself About What Happens After Pregnancy

There's a lot of information out there with regards to how you should prepare for your pregnancy and what you need to do in order to have a healthy one, but there are very few people who to talk about what happens after labor.

Let me say this, labor isn't a cakewalk, and neither are the few days after. Whether you have a vaginal birth, or you opted for C-section, you will have stitches, and stitches take time to heal.

While a vaginal birth may be easier to deal with because you don't need to worry about holding or nursing your baby, you are going to have trouble when you want to pee.

A C-section will be a little tougher for you to deal with because your stitches will hurt, and breastfeeding could be challenging.

Breastfeeding may look simply, but it is something you need time to get used to. Prepare yourself for sore nipples for the initial few weeks.

A quick tip before you get into the hospital - Carry soft cotton clothes that don't stick to your body to wear on your way back from the hospital. If you're investing in nursing bras, make sure they are soft cotton nursing bras that will not irritate sore skin.

You Don't Need Too Many Things

Don't spend money on unnecessary things your baby is going to outgrow, instead look for things that are practical, cost-effective and come in handy. The most important thing you need are diapers, wet wipes, and full breasts! Don't buy too many clothes! Infants grow fast, and they will outgrow these clothes a lot faster than you think. The 0 to 3-month size lasted my baby barely month! We had so many clothes gifted to us we didn't get a chance to use them all.

If you are throwing a baby shower, have a gift registry and let people know what you need, so these things come handy. If you can ask for a breast pump, do it! It's so convenient on-the-go, and you can travel with your baby comfortably. You can even plan an outing without having to worry about nursing.

You Need A Body Pillow

Sleeping during pregnancy is one of the hardest things to do, especially if you love sleeping on your stomach. I struggled a lot because I love sleeping on my stomach and I just couldn't get myself to sleep if I couldn't get into that position. This was until I discovered the body pillow. The body pillow helped me sleep comfortably through my pregnancy, and it also gave me an illusion that I was sleeping on my stomach. The pillow also acts as a defense mechanism and prevents you from putting too much weight on your stomach while you sleep. The worst part about the body pillow is I cannot give it up even after I have delivered.

Heartburn Remedies

If this is your first pregnancy you are bound to be nervous and you would do everything in your power to enhance your comfort level and keep your baby safe. My husband went crazy whenever I'd suffer from heartburn, and he would make sure I could on the best antacid tablets available at the drugstore.

One day I happened to come across an antacid liquid bottle and decided to try it out. I couldn't see my husband going crazy looking for the antacid tablets each week. As it turned out the antacid liquid worked perfectly, and it cured my heartburn instantly.

Quick tip - Trust your gut and do not opt for overly expensive products, unless recommended by the doctor.

Do Not Get Frustrated

It is very common for you to get frustrated within the first couple of months of pregnancy. It's a journey, and there are times you want the nine months to go by quickly. If such feelings creep in, you should focus on the fact that you are part of a miracle. A new life growing inside you is an amazing experience, and you should keep reminding yourself that you are part of it.

Stay Active

This is one thing I made sure I did during my pregnancy term. Giving birth is a difficult physical experience, and you need to be in good shape, or it will take a toll on you.

There are various ways you can stay fit. You could try yoga, or you could go for a walk daily or even ride a bike if your doctor says it's fine. You need to realize that your body is changing and not staying active will make the transition process tougher. Continue with your normal life until the third trimester, and make sure you do not succumb to the physical exertion pregnancy brings along with it.

Remember, while it's good to stay fit and exercise regularly, always consult your doctor before choosing an activity. While it's rare, some women are advised bed rest during their pregnancy.

Spend A Lot of Time Enjoy Yourself

While this is easier said than done, you need to keep taking a break from stressing about pregnancy all the time and just be you.

You need to continue living your social life and make sure you have a lot of fun with your friends and family members. This will help lift your spirits, and your mindset will be positive and happy during your pregnancy. Do everything you loved doing; however, stay within the boundaries and do not let it harm your child.

Chapter 2:
Get Your Pregnancy Off to A Good Start

Pregnancy is a massive responsibility on your shoulders. You need to take care of yourself as well as the health of your child. From the day you learn you're pregnant, you need to make sure you focus on a healthy pregnancy. The only way you would be able to do that is if you take care of your health. There are various other benefits of leading a healthy lifestyle, and I will talk about those benefits later in the book. You need to take care of your well-being, and it all begins with the first trimester. Here are a few things you need to do in order to get your pregnancy off to a good start.

Prenatal Care

You need to enroll for prenatal care and consult your doctor as soon as you learn you're pregnant. Look for non-invasive prenatal tests or NIPT to make sure your pregnancy is healthy. NIPT helps in detecting Patau syndrome, Edward's syndrome, and Down's syndrome. Initially, NIPT was recommended only for women above a certain age because they were considered high risk. However, these days the NIPT is recommended for all pregnant women.

Stay Healthy During Your Pregnancy

It's important for you to make sure you stay healthy during your pregnancy if you want a healthy baby. There are few things you can and cannot eat so educate yourself with regards to what you should and shouldn't include in your diet. Smoking and drinking are something you must let go of, and this includes second-hand smoking. If your partner smokes, you need to convince him to quit or not smoke when he is around you. Avoid bending as much as possible because this is not healthy to your baby.

Take Prenatal Vitamins

There are several vitamins you need to take when you're pregnant. Make sure you take all of these on time and on a regular basis. Folic acid is vital, and it is something you must carry on for at least the first three months depending on what your doctor suggests. I started taking Folic acid even before I was pregnant. I also had Calcium and Iron supplements during my pregnancy to help with better fetal development.

Exercise

Exercising is important during pregnancy unless advised otherwise. Not only does it help keep your body active, but it changes your mood. The best part about being pregnant in today's date is you will find tons of pregnancy classes around you, and you should enroll in them. These classes are specifically designed for pregnant women and help them stay fit and active during the nine months of pregnancy while taking precautions for the baby. I did yoga until my eighth month of pregnancy to stay healthy, and this worked wonders during my delivery because it helped me stay relaxed and calm through the pain.

When you're pregnant, always look out for signs your body gives out and if you can't handle any exercise or if you find it difficult to do, don't push yourself too much. It's important to move but not to the extent that you put strain on your baby or on your body.

Plan Birthing in Advance

Some women prefer a vaginal birth without any assisted procedures while others choose an epidural or even schedule a C-section. There is nothing wrong with any method of delivery you choose if you are confident about it. Consult your doctor and ask them about the pros and cons of the various delivery options you can pick from. You should also discuss with your partner whether they would like to be present during the delivery. I had my husband with me throughout my labor. While most women want their husband with them during delivery, some might not be comfortable with their husbands being around.

If you are not comfortable wearing hospital clothes, make sure you talk to your doctor in advance and inform them about what you would like to wear. Educate yourself with regards to the various complications that might arise and how to deal with it.

Educate Yourself

You probably have heard many women tell you different stories about what they experienced during labor but is always better for you to experience it the first hand. If you can get your hands-on birthing videos, you may want to check them out just so you know what you are getting into. I am not saying it isn't painful, because it is. But it is not something you can't handle, and when the time comes, you will get all the power to push your baby and bring him or her into this world. The more you learn about delivery and post-delivery, the more it is going to benefit you because you will handle your pregnancy better and with more confidence.

Kegels Is Your Friend

Kegels exercises help to strengthen your pelvic muscles and help you control your bladder. It's great for your uterus especially when your baby is growing in it. Kegel exercises makes your pregnancy much easier, and it helps to uterus adjust with the changes more conveniently. I practiced Kegels throughout my pregnancy, and I still do it! It's a great way to help your uterus get back to normal after delivery. Here is how it's done.

- Try holding back your urine and then release.

- Hold for another 3 seconds then release and then for another 3 seconds and then release.

- Repeat this process a total of 10 times in one go.

Do this as many times as possible during the day because it's beneficial. It's better to do it when you are sitting as it applies more pressure and it makes your pelvic muscles stronger.

Change Your Chores

The tasks you do on a regular basis may need to change once you are pregnant. Exposure to toxic chemicals such as bathroom cleaning agents and acid is something you need to stay away from. You also need to avoid heavy lifting so those trips to the grocery market may need to decrease or you'll have to be accompanied by someone every time you go. Never ever get on a step stool or on a ladder when you are pregnant as this can be very dangerous.

You also must make it a habit to sit as often as possible. Standing for long durations is not good for your baby. Bending is also not recommended, so try to keep anything that you need at a higher level. Try to avoid using the bathtub when you are pregnant especially during the later months. I remember going out for a holiday with my husband and not being able to get out of the bathtub because I was too scared it would be slippery and I may fall.

Track Your Weight

You can't afford to stay in shape when you are pregnant, and you must gain weight. A healthy weight gain is anywhere between 25 and 35 pounds. Anything above that is usually overweight, and anything below is considered underweight. Calculate your ideal weight and try attaining that weight in order to stay healthy.

Invest in Good Shoes

Trust me when I say this, you need the best possible pair of shoes when you are pregnant. Forget those dazzling slim pairs you enjoy wearing and look for something comforting. Let's not forget, you need to stay off heels when you're pregnant. You can also switch to therapeutic slippers because these can help you feel comforted and relaxed.

Get Regular Massages

Make sure you comfort yourself as much as possible when you are pregnant, and this involves therapeutic spa treatments as well. Remember, you can't get into a hot tub or a sauna that's too warm. The massages should be relaxing. Look for something that involves a calming and soothing oil to help relax you. Don't go in for painful massages during your pregnancy. Look for ones that help your body feel energized and revitalized.

Indulge in The Things You Love

If you think you're busy being pregnant, wait until the baby comes. If you want to make sure you stay relaxed during your pregnancy you should go ahead and do the things you feel you may miss out on once your baby is here.

Try sleeping for a minimum of 8 hours every night. If your sleep is not regular, then you need to make sure you consult your doctor for remedies. Listen to a lot of soothing music to help calm your nerves and go for long walks in the evening along with your partner. Do things you enjoy, such as getting a manicure or going for a fun dinner with your girl gang. The reason you need to indulge during your pregnancy is you should have no regrets about missing out when the baby is here. FOMO (fear of missing out) is a major issue these days and can get people depressed.

Consult Your Doctor Regularly

If it's your first pregnancy, there will be a lot of bodily changes that may confuse you. There are lots of twitches and aches you will feel during your first term, and you need to make sure all of these are normal. If this is your second pregnancy and you are experiencing something new, that is also a good reason for you to dial your doctor's number. Some of the things you should be concerned about include:

- Severe pain in the back

- Strong cramps at different times of the day

- Painting as well as dizziness

- Vaginal discharge

- Palpitations

- Breathing difficulty

- Constant vomiting

- Very little baby activity

- Swelling of the joints

If you have experienced any of these problems or you are experiencing something new, make sure you contact your doctor as soon as possible.

Travel Carefully

Flying is usually a tricky situation for most pregnant women. The best times to fly are different for different women, and you need to consult your doctor before you take off to for a weekend trip or to visit your relatives for a few weeks.

Ideally, the weeks between 14 and 28 are safest to fly, but no travel plan should be made without checking for two things - the approval of your doctor as well as airline restrictions. If you are cleared to fly, make sure you stock up on a lot of water, so you stay hydrated during the flight. If it is a long flight, make sure that you get up and take a walk every half an hour or so to make sure that there are no blood clots forming. Always opt for an aisle seat. This will give you more room to sit, and it will also make it easier to go to the bathroom and walk around when needed.

Rely on Sunscreen

When I was pregnant, the one thing I realized was my skin was very sensitive. This made me prone to dark patches, sunburn and spots appearing on my face. The one thing I did was apply sunscreen with SPF of 30 or even higher. I always look for creams which were chemical free. Apart from sunscreen I also made sure I always wore sunglasses and a hat. No one told me a tan could affect my baby, but I was not taking any chances. When you're pregnant, your skin tends to get sensitive, so you need to pay extra attention to your skin.

Seafood

I loved eating fish when I was pregnant. I read somewhere that pregnant women who eat fish would often end up delivering babies with a higher IQ. While that was an added incentive, I just loved eating fish because it tastes great.

Fish has high Omega 3 content. This is important for your baby's brain development. However, the one thing that you should keep in mind is to watch what kind of fish you eat. There are certain fish that have Mercury, and this can be toxic to you as well as the baby. I played it safe and stuck to my favorite fish such as Salmon, canned tuna and catfish. The fish you need to avoid shark, swordfish and king mackerel.

Eat Lots of Fruit

If caffeine was your best friend before your pregnancy, you need to find a new one, and that can be fruits. It is very difficult to give up on the caffeine addiction, but fruits help to lift energy levels, and I found that bananas along with apples were helpful. The natural sugar in fruits are the perfect substitute for caffeine, and they are extremely healthy as well.

Folate-Rich Food

When you are pregnant, you need to make sure you drink a lot of water daily. My magic number was between 8 to 10 glasses daily. Apart from drinking a lot of water, you need to eat at least five well-balanced meals throughout the day. These meals need to be folate-rich such as asparagus, fortified cereals, oranges, wheat germ, lentils, and orange juice. The Folic acid from these foods are critical for the development of the baby, and it is also important in the formation of red blood cells. To sum up, here are a few things I learned from my pregnancy, and I want you to take note.

- Always wear comfortable shoes, so you don't trip or fall

- Wear a seatbelt and sit away from the airbag

- Don't take medication without consulting your doctor

- Stay away from alcohol and smoking. Stay away from people when they smoke

Mindful Pregnancy for New Moms

- Stay away from caffeine products and products that have artificial colors

- Drink plenty of water

- Pee as often as you need to

- Relax your feet to prevent ankle swelling. Sit with your legs raised up as often as possible and soak them in warm water to ease the pain

- Sleep for at least 8 hours and take a nap if you are still tired

Chapter 3:
Morning Sickness No More

Every pregnant woman knows about morning sickness, but they are not sure how to control it or what to expect. Different women react to hormonal changes in their body in different ways. These changes are due to the development of the baby in the womb and it can create a lot of havoc in your body during pregnancy. One of these changes happens to be morning sickness. The term morning sickness itself is misleading because it is usually nausea and vomiting that doesn't necessarily happen in the morning.

While there's little you can do to avoid it completely, I have figured out a few things that can help you understand why you could be suffering from this sickness and what could trigger it so you can try to control it. While almost 70% of women complain of vomiting as well as nausea, there are some women who get through pregnancy without experiencing it at all. From my experience with pregnant women these are the kind of women more likely to suffer from morning sickness:

- A woman is carrying twins or triplets.

- A woman who has a history of morning sickness in the family.

- A woman who has experienced such sickness during their previous pregnancies.

- A woman who usually suffer from motion sickness or migraines.

There are several remedies to treat morning sickness, and you need to figure out which one suits your body best.

Never Stay on An Empty Stomach

Many pregnant women will tell you that when they had an empty stomach, it made their sickness worse. If you do not have an appetite, make sure you eat small meals but eat it regularly throughout the day. This helps lower the chances of morning sickness.

Also, when you continue eating every couple of hours, you make sure your sugar levels and blood pressure stay in control. The best thing to do is keep a lot of bland snacks at hand if you feel the urge to nibble.

Protein-Rich Food

During pregnancy, you should try and eat food that a simple and rich in protein. Protein-rich foods ensure you do not suffer an uneasy feeling in your stomach, and you are able to digest your food properly. You should also eat foods that are rich in vitamin B because this will help keep away the nauseating feeling.

Trying to incorporate as many nuts as possible in your diet and keep away foods that are spicy, rich, fried or acidic in nature. These foods will create an uneasy feeling in your stomach, and you will feel like throwing up more often.

Eat Cold Meals

Don't get excited after reading this! Cold cut meats like Ham or Salami should be avoided during pregnancy because of a possible bacterial infection from these foods.

You need to focus on eating cold meals to take care of your morning sickness. The reason cold meals are preferred over hot meals is that there are women that cannot handle the smell of cooking and they feel nauseated. If cold meals are not helping, then you should consult your doctor, and he will be able to suggest a diet to keep the morning sickness away.

Eat an Early Breakfast

If you have the habit of popping out of bed and rushing to brush your teeth, then you need to stop that habit once you are pregnant. One of the biggest causes of morning sickness is getting out of bed when your stomach is empty. Make a habit of eating a snack in bed and then try getting up very slowly. Something as small as toast can also help prevent morning sickness.

Maintain A Diary

The one thing that helped me get over my sickness was to maintain a diary and note down the peak hours of sickness and the times I felt better. This diary will help the doctor see any trends in your sickness, and he will be able to prescribe medication or even a solution to help get rid of your sickness. Even if you don't want to consult a doctor for your morning sickness, you should go ahead and analyze the diary and see what the best times to eat or drink are. It will also help identify your triggers.

Monitor Your Fluid Intake

While drinking a lot of water is good during pregnancy you should avoid drinking when you are eating a meal. Some women find it very difficult to keep the fluid down, and this can also end up with a vomiting sensation. Do not use this as an excuse for not drinking water when you are not eating. As I said before, drinking about 8 to 10 glasses of water daily is what you should aim at.

Rest A Lot

Every pregnant woman should get at least 8 hours of uninterrupted sleep. Take a quick nap whenever you can because tiredness can often make your sickness worse. However, do not make it a habit to take a lot of naps throughout the day because this will just make you lazy and you will not be able to keep your body active. Too much napping during the day could also be the reason you can't sleep properly at night.

Keep Lemons Around

This may be an old wives' tale, but it works wonders. Smelling a lemon whenever I got a nauseating feeling helped to control it and over a period it helped to prevent the feeling completely. You can also try adding lemon slices to your water or to your iced tea.

Keep Lots of Ginger Handy

Ginger is an amazing ingredient to help your nausea. Adding a little bit of ginger to your morning cup of tea can help settle your stomach. You can also try making ginger syrup or purchasing ginger capsules or tablets from your local pharmacy. You should, however, make sure you consume ginger in moderation as too much of it will result in your throat irritation.

Pregnancy Multivitamins

Although I've said multivitamins help with your health as well as your baby's development, you should know that multivitamins will also control your feelings of nausea. Even if it helps moderately, you should still go ahead and take these multivitamins daily. Irrespective of whether your morning sickness is controlled or not multivitamins should never stop.

Visit A Therapist

There are several therapists who specialize in treating women during their pregnancy. You should go in for aromatherapy or reflexology. These therapies can help you cope and emerge from your sickness.

Sharing Helps

Finally, you could try sharing your feelings with your family members and friends, so they understand what you are going through. Try speaking to somebody who has experienced pregnancy in the past.

She might be able to tell you what remedies you could take or what worked for her. Always make sure you consult your doctor before you begin any kind of medication for your morning sickness. What works for someone else may not necessarily work for you. You need to find a solution that suits your body perfectly, and this can be done when you take the time to understand your body.

Chapter 4:
Nutrition and Food (Must Know Secrets)

Pregnancy is a very important stage in a couple's life because there are more than two lives involved. While it is easy for the partners to see and take care of each other's health, it is very difficult to know what's happening in the womb, and how the baby is coping.

While there are a lot of tests and check UPS that happen on a regular basis to make sure the baby is developing, you need to make sure you take certain precautions and ensure the fetal development is healthy, and there are no hiccups along the way.

There are two components when it comes to making sure you and your baby are healthy. One is the kind of food you eat, and the other is the care you take in terms of vitamins, regular checkups, and tests. Here is my list of the best foods to eat during pregnancy and the best vitamins you can take to help your baby develop in the right manner. You should also check with your doctor with regards to which of these foods and vitamins are perfect for you.

Foods to Eat When You Are Pregnant

Almost every doctor will tell you that you need to eat foods rich in Folic acid, Vitamin D and iron. These three supplements are crucial for your health as well as the development of your baby. The supplements also ensure the cognitive development of the baby happens as per expectations. Everyone wants a baby that's perfectly healthy and intelligent, and these are the foods you should include in your diet to take a step towards a healthy pregnancy.

Green leafy vegetables are healthy irrespective of whether you are pregnant or not. However, the Folic acid in this leafy veggie is important to help with the baby's brain development. Eating the right kind of fruits and vegetables will ensure your baby is protected from any kind of tissue damage. One thing you should remember is to maintain hygiene and wash all fruits and vegetables before you cut into them. This prevents any kind of germ infection, and it will also ensure you and your baby are safe.

When you eat leafy vegetables rich in Folic acid, it reduces any kind of neural tube defects. It also eliminates the risk of a cleft lip as well as all kinds of heart defects that happen in the womb. Eating leafy vegetables also reduces the risk of preeclampsia.

Fish

You may think I love fish because I recommended this before, but certain kinds of fish are highly beneficial for your health and that of your child. Certain fish have high Omega 3 content, and they help with increasing the baby's intelligence level. Fish such as oysters also help with improving the iodine levels in pregnant women while Salmon helps of the brain development of the baby. You should also be careful about the kind of fish you should avoid, and I will talk about this a little later.

Blueberries

Antioxidants are crucial for health, and this is especially true when it comes to pregnant women. Blueberries are very high in antioxidants, and they help with the cognitive development of the baby. If you live in an area where blueberries are not commonly available, you could always substitute them with raspberries, strawberries, beans, tomatoes or artichokes. This will help with detoxifying your body and making sure that you are clean from within.

Eggs

Eggs are extremely high in protein and very low on calories. Eating one boiled egg daily will help with the brain development as well as memory development of your child. This is because they are known to contain an amino acid known as choline.

Almonds

Almonds are said to be the healthiest nuts available because they are rich in magnesium, healthy fats, vitamin E as well as protein. Almonds are also in Omega 3 which is helpful for your baby's brain development. Eating Almonds daily will reduce the chances of defects in the baby's brain. If Almonds are not easily available, you can also consume walnuts since they are also rich in Omega 3.

Greek

It is important you surround yourself with food that is rich in proteins because this will help to keep the nerve cells healthy of your baby. Nerve damage is something that is often seen in babies, and this can be avoided by consuming food such as Greek yogurt. These probiotic foods are also helpful in the bone development of the baby, and it also helps in preventing low birth weight because it contains iodine.

Cheese

As far as cognitive development of baby goes you need to make sure that you eat foods that are rich in vitamin D. If your Vitamin D intake is low, you will need to get an extra dose of cheese daily to make sure that the IQ level of your baby is high.

Pumpkin Seeds

Zinc is an important mineral that helps with the brain structure formation as well as the cognitive processing of the baby. Pumpkin seeds are not only high in zinc, but they also have antioxidant properties, and they have high nutritional value.

Beans

Iron is essential to help the brain development of your baby. Beans are said to be high in iron, and that's a major reason for you to consume beans regularly. If you dislike beans or they are not easily available, you can pick foods such as figs, spinach, raisins and chicken. If you eat raisins in small quantities daily, it will ensure your sugar levels are in control.

Milk

When it comes to iron, there's nothing better than milk. Milk helps in the development of all the cognitive functions and helps the brain development of the baby.

Vitamins and Nutrients

Your baby gets all the nutrition from you. This means you need to stock up on the nutrient levels in your body for two people rather than just for yourself. You need to keep taking your prenatal vitamins and eat the healthy foods mentioned above. These foods will help you during your pregnancy. You need to make sure you speak to your doctor, and get all the iodine, DHA and Vitamin D medication you need. Never start taking supplements without consulting your doctor.

Prenatal Vitamins

Prenatal vitamins are vitamins meant for pregnant women. They are better than your regular multivitamins, and they have more nutrients that help during pregnancy. You need to ask your doctor for prenatal vitamins when you go in for your prenatal checkup. You need to take the prenatal vitamins daily.

If you are planning to get pregnant, you can start your prenatal vitamins in preparation for your pregnancy. Make sure you check with your doctor before you begin consuming these vitamins.

When pregnant, your body needs all minerals and vitamins in order to stay healthy. Your baby will also rely on you for the nutrient intake. If you are pregnant with more than one baby, you will need to increase your intake of prenatal vitamins. If there are certain foods, you cannot eat or certain vitamins that are not agreeing with you. Speak with your doctor and get an alternative. Ignoring this problem is not the healthiest solution.

Important Nutrients During Pregnancy

There are several important nutrients that play an important role in the development of the baby. They are:

Folic Acid

Folic acid is crucial to the development of the body. If you start taking folic acid before you get pregnant and even during your pregnancy, you will avoid several brain defects as well as spine defects. Folic acid is also known to prevent defects such as a cleft lip or a cleft palate. Your dosage for folic acid should be decided after consultation with your doctor. Ideally, you could start taking folic acid even if you are trying to get pregnant but consuming it during pregnancy, especially during the first 12 weeks, is crucial.

Folic acid is also known to prevent neural tube defects, more commonly known as NTDs. If you have had a high-risk pregnancy in the past, you need to make sure you consume folic acid when you're planning a baby. However, you need to be careful with the number of multivitamins that you consume. Too many nutrients can also prove to be harmful to your health. My doctor helped me figure out the best solution, and you need to do that as well. You need to take folic acid if:

- Your partner already has a child with a neural tube defect (NTD).

- Any of your previous pregnancies had an NTD.

- Either of you has an NTD (you or your partner).

If you do not want to consume too many capsules, you can also eat food that is rich in folic acid. Some amazing foods include:

- Cornmeal

- Breakfast cereal

- Bread

- Pasta

- Flour

- White rice

- Beans
- Lentils
- Leafy greens such as broccoli and spinach
- Orange juice

Iron

Iron is a vital mineral in the body and is used to produce hemoglobin. Hemoglobin is critical in carrying oxygen through your entire body. If you didn't realize it yet, you need twice as much iron when you are pregnant because you are supporting two bodies. The iron from your body will also carry oxygen to your baby's body. The iron is used to create the baby's own blood. Your body needs a certain amount of iron daily when you are pregnant. Your prenatal vitamins will be able to cover the requirement. If you do not want to take any chances you can also include the following foods in your diet that are said to be excellent sources of iron:

- Poultry
- Seafood
- Lean Meat
- Leafy Greens
- Bread

- Cereal

- Raisins

- Nuts

- Beans

- Dry fruits

There are two types of iron your body absorbs. One is heme Iron, and the other is non-heme Iron. You get heme Iron from poultry, meat, and fish. You get non-heme Iron from vegetables, fruits, cereal, nuts, and beans. You receive more non-heme iron when you start eating fruits and vegetables along with your poultry, meat, and fish. You can also include a lot of food that contains vitamin C. These foods include mango, cantaloupe, grapefruit, tomatoes, broccoli, spinach, and cabbage.

If you do not give enough iron, there may be several health complications that may occur. These include:

- Anemia

- Viral infections

- Low birth weight baby

- Premature baby

Calcium

Calcium is an extremely important mineral that aids in the development of your baby's heart, teeth, bones and muscles along with nerve development. While you can get your daily dose of calcium from your prenatal vitamins, you can also consume a lot of food that will provide you with enough calcium. These foods include:

- Kale
- Broccoli
- Yogurt
- Cheese
- Milk
- Orange juice

When you do not receive enough calcium during your pregnancy term, your body takes calcium from your bones and passes it on to your baby. This can lead to severe health complications such as osteoporosis where your bones will become weak and break easily.

Vitamin D

While you need calcium daily, you also need vitamin D to help your body absorb calcium. Vitamin D helps your body's muscles, nerves, and the immune system. It is important for your baby's bones and teeth to grow, and this is where vitamin D comes into the picture. Foods that include Vitamin D are:

- Cereal

- Milk

- Fatty fish

You will also be able to absorb vitamin D when you meet the sun. However, you need to be careful because too much exposure to the sun can also cause harmful effects such as premature aging and cancer. It is best to get your vitamin D from your prenatal vitamins and foods that are mentioned above.

DHA

DHA is docosahexaenoic acid, and it is more commonly known as Omega 3 fatty acid. DHA helps with the development and growth of the baby. It is crucial for the development of the eyes and the brain as well. You should know that not all prenatal vitamins help with providing DHA to your body, so you need to consult your doctor and check if you need to take a DHA supplement apart from your prenatal vitamins. If you do not want to take any additional supplements, you can also consume foods that contain DHA. These include:

- Low mercury fish such as Trout, Salmon, Halibut, and Anchovies.

- Milk

- Orange juice
- Eggs

Iodine

Iodine is another crucial mineral your body needs. Iodine is useful in making thyroid hormones. The thyroid is present in your neck, and it helps to create hormones that assist your body in using and storing energy that it gets from food. Iodine helps the thyroid gland to make hormones and helps your body use energy efficiently. Iodine also helps to develop your baby's brain as well as the nervous system. Iodine is important for your baby's movement, thinking ability and feeling ability. Just like DHA, not all prenatal vitamins contain iodine, and therefore you need to focus on foods that contain Iodine. These include:

- Yogurt
- Milk
- Fish
- Cheese
- Fortified cereal
- Enriched bread
- Iodized salt

What to Avoid Eating and Drinking When Pregnant

I have tried everything that is to know as far as acceptable foods and drinks are concerned, but there are certain foods and beverages you should avoid when you are pregnant. I cannot keep stressing on the fact that you need to stick to a healthy diet when you are pregnant because it helps you stay healthy as well as your child develop properly.

You need to read the package for everything you purchase from your supermarket and pay close attention to everything you eat. There are certain foods you can consume on the odd occasion, while there are other foods that need to stay off the table. These are some important foods and beverages you need to stay away from or try and minimize:

High-Mercury Fish

I know I've spoken about this before, but I cannot stress enough on the fact that mercury is toxic for you as well as your baby. There is no known safe level of Mercury you can consume and therefore its best kept away. Mercury can harm your immune system, your nervous system, and your kidneys.

It is also known to create serious developmental problems to the child in the womb. If you are not sure which fish contain Mercury and which don't, you should know high Mercury fish are only found in polluted seas and are the large marine fish that are high risk. If you feel the urge to eat any of the fish that contain high Mercury, you should consult your doctor before you do. Here are the high Mercury fish you should be aware of:

- Swordfish
- Shark
- Albacore tuna
- King mackerel

Not all the fish that are found in the high seas contain a lot of Mercury. Staying away from fish will keep you away from Omega 3 fatty acids, and this is not good for your health. You need high levels of Omega 3 fatty acids, and you can get this by eating healthy fish. You can always consult your doctor if you are not sure which fish to eat.

Undercooked Fish

There are various varieties of fish that are either served undercooked or raw. Most of these fish are usually shellfish, and they are known to cause various viral as well as bacterial infections. Certain fish also contain parasites, and it is best to stay away from undercooked fish or raw fish as much as possible. Some of the infections from undercooked fish are known to only affect the mother and make her weak and dehydrated. Other infections from undercooked fish can also affect the unborn and can have fatal consequences.

Listeria is one infection that pregnant women need to be careful about. Listeria is a bacterium that is found in contaminated plants as well as water. It can infect raw fish during the processing stage or the smoking and the drying stage. When Listeria is passed to your unborn baby, it can lead to complications such as miscarriage, premature delivery, and stillbirth. This is the reason it is advised that pregnant women avoid raw fish along with shellfish as much as possible. This also includes several Sushi dishes.

Undercooked Meat, Raw Meat, and Processed Meat

Like undercooked fish and raw fish, and undercooked meat and raw meat can also increase your chances of contracting an infection. The bacteria in undercooked meat can affect your unborn and can also lead to several neurological conditions such as blindness, intellectual disabilities, and epilepsy. Most people believe that the bacteria are only found on the surface of the meat. The truth is that there are certain bacteria that are also present inside the muscle fibers. There are certain cuts of meat; however, that can be safe to consume when it is not cooked completely. These include sirloins, tenderloins as well as ribeye. Meat that should never be consumed undercooked or raw includes minced meat, burger patties, poultry, and pork. Certain deli meat, as well as hot dogs, can also contain bacteria, and these are best eaten when cooked properly. If you only have processed meat in the house and you are feeling hungry, you can consume it only after you reheat the meat in hot boiling water.

Raw Eggs

Not many people know this, but raw eggs contain Salmonella. The symptoms of Salmonella are usually experienced only by the pregnant mother and do not pass on to the baby. In very rare cases does the infection pass on to the uterus and when this happens, it could lead to premature birth or stillbirth. There are various foods that also contain raw eggs. These include:

- Poached eggs
- Scrambled eggs
- Homemade mayonnaise
- Hollandaise sauce
- Homemade ice cream
- Certain salad dressings
- Cake icing

In case you are wondering why homemade has been mentioned here, you should know that commercial products contain raw pasteurized eggs, and these are said to be safe to consume. If you crave eggs, you should only consume pasteurized and well-cooked eggs.

Organ Meat

Organ meats are a great source of vitamin A, Vitamin B12, Iron and Copper. All these minerals are great for the mother and her unborn child. However, too much animal-based Vitamin A is not recommended when you are pregnant. It causes something known as vitamin A toxicity, and this can result in liver toxicity and congenital disabilities. While organ meat is recommended for pregnant women, it should not be consumed more than once every couple of weeks. Always consult your doctor for the amount that you should consume depending on your body type.

Caffeine

Caffeine is the most commonly used substance in the world and is found in various soft drinks, tea, coffee, and cocoa. While pregnant women can consume caffeine, they should not consume more than two or three cups of coffee daily. Caffeine is usually absorbed easily, and this passes on to the placenta and the fetus. Since the placenta doesn't have the enzyme to metabolize caffeine, a high level of caffeine will build up and it will restrict fetal growth and cause low birth weight. When low birth weight occurs, there are several complications that could occur such as infant death or type 2 diabetes along with heart diseases.

Raw Sprouts

Like raw meat and raw fish, raw sprouts are also not advisable. Raw sprouts are also known to contain Salmonella. Since raw sprouts require a humid environment to start sprouting, it is perfect for

Salmonella to breed and it is next to impossible to wash off this bacterium. When you are pregnant, it is best to avoid raw sprouts. Sprouts that have been cooked are safe to consume, and you should not stay away from them.

Unwashed Food

Have you ever been in such a hurry that you see an apple in your fruit basket, and you pick it up and start munching on it? You need to avoid doing that when you're pregnant. When you eat fruits or vegetables without peeling or washing them, there are several parasites as well as bacteria that you would be consuming. These parasites and bacteria are usually passed onto the fruits and vegetables through the soil or through the handling of the produce. The bacteria found on unwashed and unpeeled fruits and vegetables are said to be dangerous for the mother as well as the baby. One of the most dangerous parasites called Toxoplasma is found on unwashed fruits and vegetables. Several people get affected by Toxoplasmosis on a regular basis, and most of them feel no symptoms. Most of the infants that are infected with this parasite do not show any symptoms when they are born. However, intellectual disabilities, as well as blindness, may creep in at a later stage in life. A very small percentage of newborns that are infected with Toxoplasma suffer from brain damage at birth.

Unpasteurized Dairy and Fruit Juices

Unpasteurized cheese and raw milk contain a lot of harmful bacteria, and it's the same with unpasteurized juice. All the infections caused by the bacteria found in unpasteurized products can have life-threatening consequences for your baby. Pasteurization is the safest way to kill any kind of bacteria and retain nutritional value. When you are pregnant, it is advisable to only consume pasteurized products especially cheese, milk and fruit juices.

Alcohol

It goes without saying pregnant women should stay away from alcohol completely because it increases the risk of stillbirth and even a miscarriage. While some women feel that a small amount of alcohol on a weekly basis does no harm, they are wrong. The baby's brain development gets impacted by even the smallest amount of alcohol. It is said to cause fetal alcohol syndrome that includes heart defects, facial deformities, and intellectual disabilities. There is no reason to drink alcohol when you are pregnant, and you should avoid it completely.

Processed Junk Food

When you are pregnant, you only need to think about nutrients and calories because it is needed for you and your baby's growth. Your baby needs all the protein, nutrients, iron and folate that it can get. Unlike common thinking, you do not need to eat twice as much because you are eating for two. You just need to eat healthy and eat foods that contain a lot of protein and nutrients. Try to eat whole foods as much as possible because it helps to fulfill the needs of your child as well as your health needs. When you consume processed junk food, you are consuming a lot of sugar, calories and added fat. The nutrient value for junk food is usually very low, and it is best to stay away from this as much as possible. When you consume added sugar that has been added to processed junk food, it increases the risk of several diseases including heart complications as well as type 2 diabetes. It's important to gain weight when you are pregnant; however, excessive weight can lead to various diseases as well as complications. It can increase the risk of gestational diabetes as well as birth complications.

Chapter 5:
Approved Exercises

There is no denying that it is healthy for you to exercise when you are pregnant, but that doesn't mean you should exercise the way you used to, prior to being pregnant. There are a ton of exercises that you should and shouldn't carry out during your pregnancy. You need to figure out which exercises can help you get through these nine months with ease and which ones you should stay away from.

While it is healthy for you to exercise while pregnant, it is also important for you to make sure you consult your doctor to get a go-ahead to exercise.

While most women have a healthy pregnancy and this allows them to stay active for the nine months, there are few situations where certain complications may not allow you to exercise during your pregnancy. You also need to remember that there are different kinds of exercises for each trimester. So, as you grow into your pregnancy, you may need to lower the intensity of the exercise you do and move to calming exercises such as yoga to help prepare your body.

If you have never exercised in your life, and you have been advised to do so during pregnancy, then stick to something basic like walks. However, if you were active and you would like to maintain your fitness levels, then you can opt-in for something more intense, depending on what your body can handle.

Body Changes

When you're pregnant your body is going to go through a lot of changes physically, and therefore you need to accommodate an exercise regime you are comfortable with. Apart from the fact that you will gain weight, it is not recommended for you to run because it could be harmful for your baby. Pregnant women gain a lot of weight around the belly area and the body balance changes making it more difficult to you to stay confident on your feet which is why sudden movements and fast exercises it should be done at a considerably slower pace. Walking is an easy and great way to keep your entire body active during your pregnancy.

When exercising remember not to indulge in any exercise that accelerates your heart rate or exhausts you too much because this isn't good for your child. Any exercise that makes you feel dizzy or lightheaded should also be avoided. If you are wondering what exercises are safe during pregnancy, then below is a list of some exercises most of my friends did during their pregnancy term. I say this again, before you start exercising make sure you speak to your doctor, so you know what you are doing it safely for your baby.

Usually, women who have a low-risk pregnancy shouldn't exercise for more than 30 minutes a day for a maximum of 4 days a week. A low-risk pregnancy is a pregnancy that is not constrained by your doctor, and you have no complications.

Every individual is different, and during your pregnancy, you will experience changes that may be unique to your body which is why you need to check your intensity levels and come up with an exercise regime you are comfortable with without stressing your child in any manner. A lot of people wonder what moderate intensity exercises are. This simply defines your level of fitness and how much you can moderately handle. For some women, a 30-minute walk is defined as a moderate exercise while for others it could be much longer.

If you have aches in your joints, do not put too much pressure on them during exercise because this might make it worse. The best way to begin a healthy exercise routine is to always warm up and then cool it down post the exercise. It's difficult for a pregnant woman to be flexible and trust me, even stretching a little would make me feel like a balloon about to pop. So, everything you do needs to be done gently and slowly. Yoga is great, and I did it for a long time during my pregnancy, so I know just how much it helped me relax. However, I stuck to the basic yoga positions that weren't too complicated because I didn't want to attempt something that could result in an injury. The simple stretches can help you through your pregnancy, and apart from keeping your body healthy, it helps your pelvic muscles adjust to the baby growing inside.

Walking

Another way to exercise during pregnancy is walking which is also the safest. Most pregnant women believe that since they are only walking, they need to walk briskly and fast, so they stay healthy and fit. Let me remind you, when you are pregnant, you will not have the best balance. So, whatever you do, do it slowly. Walking briskly not only risks exertion but it also increases the chances of falling. If you think that a 30-minute walk is too little, increase the time that you walk but don't increase your pace. Walking too fast can also cause cramps in your body which will make it extremely uncomfortable to deal with. When you start walking, do it very slowly and gradually increase your pace to something that's not too fast but not too slow either.

Water Sports

Swimming in water is super fun when you're pregnant because it helps to maintain your body temperature and increases your fitness levels. There isn't too much risk of muscle strain when you are in the water. There is no risk of falling and losing balance as well, which is why this is a great pick. Women who suffer from backaches and leg swellings will find water activities highly beneficial. However, some women tend to get a little dizzy in the water, and if that's how you feel, then you may want to stay away from water during pregnancy.

Stationary Cycling

I spoke about cycling and major benefits it has, but it's also risky for women cycle around in a garden because there's a risk of falling. If you want to benefit from cycling during your pregnancy try getting and exercising bike which is comfortable and safe. If you choose cycling you can do it for your first two trimesters only, don't cycle during your third trimester because it puts a lot of pressure on your belly and balancing even on a stationary bike could get difficult.

Weight Training

Lifting weight during pregnancy has no risks as they are not too heavy. However, if you have never lifted weights in your life do not start when you're pregnant, it's not a great time to begin. While weight training benefits the body, it is designed specifically for pregnant women who lead an active lifestyle prior to pregnancy, and if you try doing it only once, you're pregnant, you will suffer from a lot of muscle cramping and pain.

Running

While I am completely against the idea of running during pregnancy because there's always the risk of a fall, if you have been doing this prior to getting pregnant you can continue running through your first trimester as well. However, once your belly grows, stop running because there are balance issues and falling could cause major problems in your pregnancy.

The Kind of Exercises to Avoid

Exercising is extremely safe and is something that every pregnant woman should do. However, there are several exercises that increase the risk of complications as well as injuries. Some exercises can be extremely tiring, and it can cause a lot of discomfort for the mother as well as the child. If you have always loved exercising and you want to continue that trend even when you are pregnant then you need to make a note of the following exercises that need to be avoided:

Heavy Weight Training

Heavy weight training is something that should be avoided when you are pregnant. When you lift heavy weights, it puts a lot of stress on your musculoskeletal system as well as your cardiovascular system.

Breath Holding

There are certain exercises that require you to hold your breath for a certain amount of time. Yoga along with weight training, are classic examples where you need to control the way you breathe, and this is something that can cause a lot of stress. If any of your exercises require you to stop breathing at any point in time, you need to make sure that you stop those exercises immediately.

Lying on Your Back

The first trimester is extremely crucial for pregnant women, and you need to make sure you avoid any kind of exercises that involve lying on your back. When you lie on your back, the blood flow to the fetus gets affected, and this is not good for the health of your baby.

Lying on Your Stomach

Exercises that involve lying on your stomach are not safe irrespective what stage of pregnancy you are in. You need to make sure that you avoid such exercises because it would put a lot of stress on your stomach and your baby. These exercises include abdominal strengthening exercises and Pilates. Although Pilates does not involve you lying on your stomach, it does put stress on your abdomen, and it can cause muscle weakness.

Contact Sports

Intensity sports or contact sports should be avoided when you are pregnant. Sports such a soccer, ice hockey and basketball can cause a lot of stress on your abdomen and can result in abdominal trauma.

Standing Still

There are certain exercises that require you to stand still for long periods. Such exercises should be avoided because it affects the blood pressure and it could put a lot of stress on your baby.

Scuba Diving

Scuba diving is done under very high pressure, and this should be avoided because it has resulted in various congenital disabilities as well as fetal decompression sickness.

Falling

Any sports or exercises that require you to run around with the possibility of falling should be avoided. Sports such as tennis and racquetball are best kept away when you are pregnant.

Altitude Sports

Any sports that are done at high altitudes need to be avoided because this can result in reduced oxygen supply to your baby. Altitude of up to 2500 meters are considered safe however if you experience any kind of altitude sickness, chest pain, shortness of breath or lightheadedness, you need to stop the exercise immediately and consult your doctor.

It goes without saying that you need to consult with your doctor before you begin any kind of physical activity. Being physical is important but putting a strain on you and your baby is not recommended.

Chapter 6:
Money Saving Hacks for Maternity Clothing

Pregnancies are exciting, and most women end up spending a ton of money on maternity clothes they never look back at. Instead of purchasing too many maternity clothes you never use post-delivery here are some interesting hacks I came up with that benefited me through my pregnancy.

Bodysuits

I don't like showing my skin, and I hated it when I was pregnant because my belly kept protruding and pushing my t-shirt a little higher. Bodysuits work wonders because they helped hide my belly and cover it up effectively. It was also comfortable because you don't feel exposed and you can even choose to combine it with a sweater or jacket and add a little style.

If you have a ton of bodysuits in your closet, your pregnancy is the perfect time to make use of them. They stretch perfectly and move according to your body shape making you comfortable in what you wear. Is also a great way to look a little slimmer during your pregnancy?

Bra Extenders

You gaining weight means your bra will get tighter. If you haven't increased in cup size, you don't need to get rid of your old bra and replace it with a new one. I just purchased a few standard bras and was able to wear the existing bras through most of my pregnancy. I decided to invest in nursing bras only after my baby was born only because it was more convenient to breastfeed. Through my pregnancy, I used the same bras that I used prior to getting pregnant.

Using A Hair Tie for Your Jeans

This one may seem a little embarrassing to share, but I am guilty of doing it until my sixth month of pregnancy. I used a hair tie and hooked it inside the slit to accommodate my growing belly to still get the button done. I wore long tops to cover up this hack, but it's kind of benefited me and I didn't have to invest in multiple jeans throughout my pregnancy. It was only during my last trimester that I bought maternity pants. Trust me when I say this, get yourself one black pair of jeans and any other color you think will blend in with your wardrobe perfectly. You don't have to choose expensive branded ones. Even if you get maternity pants at your local store, purchase them because you don't have to deal with them for a long time.

String Bikini

Just because you're pregnant doesn't mean you have to avoid the beach. String bikinis are amazing because you can wear them throughout your pregnancy, and you can just customize the strings as and when you need to. I headed out for a holiday with three pairs a string bikini that I had from my honeymoon. All I did was extend the size of the strings.

Dresses

Maternity dresses gained a lot of popularity back in the 80's. To me, they still look like night dresses that women wear in public. There are dresses that you can purchase and use post pregnancy as well. A t-shirt dress is a classic example of something you can use during your pregnancy and post it. T-shirt dresses look cute, and you can pair them with flat shoes and sneakers to add to your attire. You can also look for stretchable fabric that goes snug around your belly. These dresses can be used post-delivery and still look stylish. Just because you're pregnant doesn't mean you can't look good in what you wear, you just need to make sure you get your hands and clothes that are not labeled as 'maternity clothes.

Sock Boots

Dealing with winters during your pregnancy could get a little difficult if you got a pair of boots that don't fit because of your feet swelling. If you want to invest in shoes, try to get the ones that have a sock built inside of it. This way you can make use of the boots even after your pregnancy because they will never be too big since they are flexible.

Oversized Coats

Jackets and coats look great when they are a size bigger, and when you are pregnant it will fit you just right. This makes it a great choice to invest in during pregnancy.

Quick tip - Don't overindulge in jackets and coats and stick to about one or maximum two that you can use. Pregnant women tend to feel a lot hotter, so you won't be wearing a jacket as much.

Protecting Your Belly Button

There are several expensive clothes that are meant to take care of your sensitive belly button. Rather than spending on such expensive clothes, you can take care of your belly button and make sure that it does not touch any of your fabric. When you reach towards the end of your pregnancy, your belly button will start protruding outward. One of the best things to do is to use a silicone nipple cover and put it on your belly button. This will make sure that your belly button does not rub against your clothing and it does not protrude through your top. There are various silicon options that are available in deep skin tones as well.

Tops That Grow with You

It's hard to believe that there are tops that can grow with you. If you feel that your breasts are growing very large or your stomach is growing rapidly, you can purchase tops that you can tie. This can be done by tying a few of your old scarfs together and making a shirt. This is a perfect kind of clothing to use when it is extremely hot outside, and you will not even have to worry about the shirt not fitting you. All you need to do is tie it around your breasts, and you will be comfortable walking around in the hot sun. Don't forget to apply sunscreen on your belly because this will help protect you and your baby.

Polyester Pajamas

If you have been applying oil or any kind of lotion on your stomach to prevent stretch marks, most of your cotton pajamas will get ruined because they soak up the oil as well as lotions. The best thing to do is to take out your polyester pajamas because they will not soak up anything. All you need to do is wear them when you sleep and wash them when you wake up and it will be as good as new. Using polyester pajamas are a lot more comfortable and an economic option.

Adjustable Bras

If your cup size does not change during your pregnancy, then you can use a bra extender, as I mentioned above. However, if your cup size changes constantly then you will need adjustable bras to keep you comfortable throughout your pregnancy. There are several adjustable bras that are available, and they even come with the nursing option as well as a workout option. You can choose one to depend on what you want to use it for. If you plan on using your bra even after you deliver your baby, then you may want to invest in the adjustable nursing bra.

Don't Invest in Shoes with Laces

For someone that has already gone through a pregnancy, let me tell you that bending over to tie your shoes is extremely difficult and almost next to impossible. It is not even recommended by your doctor, and the only way you can avoid this is by purchasing shoes that you can slip on. Slip-on shoes are available in various colors and various economic options so you can pick one depending on what suits your budget and your preference.

Belly Bands

Belly bands are the latest trend, and several women loves wearing these under a dress or even a loose sweater. This is done in order to avoid any kind of itchiness from the fabric and to keep your dress safe from the oil and creams that you have been applying on your belly. You can create your own belly band at home rather than investing in an expensive one. All you need to do is pull out an old pair of stockings and cut them in half. This half stocking works perfectly as a belly band accessory, and it can be worn under all your clothes.

Kinesiology Tape

The problem with a belly band is it can get curled up and look funny under a dress or a top. You can opt-in for a Kinesiology tape. This tape allows for a seamless look, and it will also support your belly and keep it away from any kind of irritation.

Chapter 7:
First Trimester Essential Secrets

Whether or not you are planning to have a baby, the minute you learn that you are pregnant, it fills your heart with a lot of joy and excitement. There are also several questions that are unanswered, and most women don't know where to start. If you are wondering how you should go through your first trimester, then here are a few secrets you should follow to enjoy your pregnancy to the fullest. Your first trimester is essential because it's the highest risk of your pregnancy and most miscarriages occur during these three months. It takes a while for your baby to latch onto your uterus firmly and that doesn't happen during the first three months. This means you must be careful and make sure you take the pregnancy to full term and avoid any complications.

Arrange an Appointment with Your Midwife

Every pregnant woman makes sure she gets to the doctor as soon as possible. However, what she doesn't remember is it's important for her to schedule a meeting with her midwife as well. Your midwife will spend more time with you during your pregnancy time than your doctor will, so the sooner you get to know here, the better it is. The best time to get to know your midwife is anywhere between the 10th to the 12th week of your pregnancy. Sometimes doctors choose to introduce the midwife to the pregnant woman even as early as the 8th week. Your first appointment with the midwife will last long because this includes a thorough examination including your lifestyle and your medical history.

Although every midwife will take note of every little detail in your life, you need to have a list ready with you to cross-check just so you are confident she's got everything covered. Some important topics you should remember to cover include

- Your medical history, including any pregnancy complications

- The lifestyle you lead

- All information regarding what you need to do during your pregnancy - including what you should eat and what exercises are safe for your baby

- Make sure to check your blood pressure

- Get your height and weight measured and calculate your body mass index

- Ask for a complete list of all the screening tests you need to go through

Start Your Prenatal Vitamins

If you weren't taking folic acid prior to the pregnancy now is the time for you to start. Once you have spoken about the various vitamins and nutrients, you need to make sure you take a complete list and ask your doctor whether you need to take them and in what dosages.

Ask Before You Take Any Medication

If you are on medication for any sickness or ailment, make sure you ask your doctor whether you can continue taking that medication or whether there is a safer alternative. People who suffer from thyroid and diabetes may need to check with the doctor about the kind of medication they are taking and whether it is safe for the baby or not. Even if you suffer from migraine or certain kind of aches in your body, make sure you ask the doctor what medicines are safe during pregnancy. If possible, get the complete list of safe medications to take and stock up, so you don't end up taking something that's not safe for you.

Quit Smoking If You Are A Smoker

Some pregnant women believe that they can continue smoking until 12 weeks before they quit smoking, but that's far from the truth. If you continue smoking, you are at a higher risk of suffering a miscarriage or any complications within the first trimester. Women that continue smoking during the first trimester are also at risk of premature labor and low birth weight. If your partner smokes, you may have to ask him to either quit smoking or smoke outside the house, so it doesn't affect you or your baby. Remember, second-hand smoke is just as bad as smoking.

Learn About the Danger Signs

It's important for you to educate yourself with regards to the symptoms of pregnancy that are normal and the ones you shouldn't ignore. Slight cramping as your stomach expands is normal, but if your cramps are a little severe like your periods bleeding along with the cramping, you may want to call your midwife or doctor immediately. Don't ignore small symptoms that are not normal, or you think they are going to fade away eventually. The sooner you act upon a signal that indicates danger, the safer you keep your baby.

Rest as Often as Possible

Pregnant women need to sleep a lot, and your first trimester is probably the most difficult time for you because you are not used to resting as much. There are times you wake up in the morning feeling fresh as ever but there will be times you may want to crawl back into bed. This is simply because of the changing hormones in your body and the fact that your body is working harder to keep the life inside you healthy. If you work a regular 9 to 5 job, make sure that you relax as much as possible during the weekends and sleep for as long as you want. If you can practice sleeping on your right side, you may want to try doing it because lying on your back may affect the blood flow to your baby and thus increases the risk of a stillborn.

Prepare to See Your Baby

If your pregnancy is normal and you have no complications, you will most probably be scheduled for an ultrasound between the 10th to the 14th week of your pregnancy. This is the time you will be able to hear your baby's heartbeat for the first time and get an approximate due date. This ultrasound usually takes about 20 minutes, but at times it may take a little longer.

Quick tip - you need to have a full bladder to get a good ultrasound. So, drink plenty of water before you head to the clinic for your scan.

Baby's Development

You need to do anything and everything possible to make sure that your baby is developing properly. While you may take certain precautions and ensure that you are consuming all your vitamins as well as nutrients, you need to follow your baby's development and make sure that the fetus is developing properly, and the heart rate is stable. There are a few apps that are available that will allow you to monitor your baby's development on a weekly basis. Make sure you consult with your doctor before you rely on any of these apps because most of these apps are fake and they may provide false information.

Join A Club

If it is your first pregnancy, there will be a lot of anxiety with regards to what to expect and what not to do. Speaking with other pregnant women may or may not help if they are not delivering in the same month as you. You need to speak with women that are at the same stage as you and would be due in the same month. Join a birth club that segregates mothers based on the delivery date, and this will help you share your experiences as well as learn from the experiences from other pregnant women.

Budgeting

While it is only the first trimester, it is important to budget for the baby and prepare a plan that will help you handle the cost of a growing child. There are a number of expenses that will keep adding up, and you need to make sure that you come up with ideas that will help you save money or look for secondary jobs that can help you increase your income.

Opt-In for A Massage

Pregnancy can be a very stressful period, and you may suffer from back aches as well as headaches. The only way to get through this stressful period is by relaxing yourself and getting a pregnancy massage. You do not need to go to a massage parlor or a spa to get a massage. You can just ask your partner to rub your shoulders along with your back and your head, and this will help relieve any stress or tension you are going through.

Involve Your Partner

Women usually connect with the child from a very early stage in the pregnancy. You will be able to experience all the symptoms and know early on if your child is healthy or not. This connection between a mother and a child is extremely close, and there is nothing that can come between that. But the one person that misses out on all this is the father. Fathers are not able to bond with the baby as much as they would like to because of obvious reasons. Try and get your partner involved in various things such as taking you for your daily walks or helping you plan with the finances or even taking you for your appointments. When the partner gets involved with everything, he will feel a lot better, and he will also try and help to create a better bond with the baby.

Antenatal Classes

When you get pregnant, there are several antenatal classes that you need to look up in your area. These classes get full very quickly, and you need to make sure that you book your classes as early as possible. If you have been planning your pregnancy, it is better to check out antenatal classes even before your pregnancy is confirmed. Most of the classes will enroll you even if you are anticipating your pregnancy in the coming months. It is better to start these classes rather than let your first trimester go by without you knowing how to cope with parenthood as well as labor and childbirth.

Floor Exercises

One of the things that your antenatal classes will teach you is pelvic floor exercises. These exercises will prevent you from leaking while you walk. If you've not been shown how to do the pelvic floor exercises during your antenatal classes, you can always contact your midwife, and she will help you with the same. It is important to continue with pelvic floor exercises during the first semester because this will help your body prepare in the right manner for the rest of your pregnancy.

Household Chores

Household chores are something that cannot be avoided; however, you need to make sure that you stay away from cleaning products as well as chemicals. As stated before, chemicals are very harmful to you and your baby and the fumes that emerge from these can have serious repercussions on your unborn child. One of the things that you should do is keep all your windows open when you are cleaning your house. You should also avoid any products that are available in aerosol cans. If you are a nurse or you work in an area that can expose you to X-rays, then you need to consider changing your job because X-rays are not good for you or your baby.

Exercise

Like I said, exercising in moderation can help you cope with the mental as well as physical demands during your pregnancy. However, you need to be sure that you are as comfortable as possible when you are exercising. While some women try to keep up with their exercising habits even when they are pregnant, you need to make sure that you stay active only by staying within the limits of your comfort.

Announcing Your Pregnancy

Catherine Taylor

The first trimester is not only exciting and crucial for the parents, but it is also very exciting for the immediate family members. Some couples do not like to announce their baby until the second trimester because by then the bump becomes very difficult to hide. While it is your choice when to announce your pregnancy, you may want to reveal it during the first semester if you are involved in a job that is dangerous or strenuous. Getting support from family members is extremely crucial during a tough time, and your friends at work can also help you if your job could be potentially dangerous to you or your baby. Talk to your partner and decide when the right time to announce the pregnancy is, depending on the complications with your pregnancy or the complications involving your job.

Chapter 8:
Second Trimester Essential Secrets

Once you're in your second trimester, your baby has secured itself in your womb, and this is around the time you should start getting a little more involved with various activities related to your pregnancy to have a healthy one. Here are a few to do's you should get tick off your list during your second trimester.

Prenatal Exercise Classes

While you should ideally sign up with these classes in your first trimester, if you haven't already done this you may want to do so now. The classes will not only help you stay fit but prepare you for labor. The reason these classes are so beneficial is that you come across other pregnant women and it becomes easier for you to discuss your problems with people who are going to the same bodily changes as you are.

Learn About Your Prenatal Visits

You must visit your midwife at least once a month during your second trimester just to make sure you are healthy, and your blood sugar and pressure is normal. This is also the time you could do a screen test for down syndrome and other forms or abnormalities in the baby. Genetic disorders and neural tube defects are also usually detected in this trimester. Your ultrasound during the second trimester is something you will thoroughly enjoy because you will be able to see what your baby looks like as he or she takes form.

Make Changes to Your Wardrobe

You don't have to go shopping for maternity clothes and like I discussed in chapter 6, make smart choices and make sure that you have clothes that you are comfortable in.

Decide Whether You Need A Professional Labor Coach

Labor coaches have become popular these days, and a lot of women are hiring them to help with the process of labor and delivery. Labor coaches provide you with a lot of emotional support as well as guidance that helps you get through labor in a more relaxed and comfortable manner. It is always best to have one during the second trimester because you start connecting with them and you manage to discuss the position for delivery you are comfortable with and every little detail about going into labor with ample time in hand. While a lot of people leave having a labor coach for the third trimester, if your baby is premature it will be difficult for your labor coach to assist you because of lack of time.

Plan Adult Time

Once you enter your second trimester your symptoms will probably ease, and you might become more sexually active. It's during these months that you should make the most of your relationship with your partner. Try going out on a date and enjoying being a couple just before the baby arrives so you can feel complete and happy and prepared for the baby even more. It's also important to get intimate with your partner because it helps you feel sexy, and it helps you overcome any doubts you have about your body because of the number of changes that you go through. This is a great time to plan a babymoon because it is safe to travel, and your belly isn't very big, so you'll be able to move around more comfortably.

Start Moisturizing Your Belly
If you want to stay away from stretch marks, you must moisturize your belly as often as possible. As your belly grows, your skin starts to stretch, and it increases the urge to start itching. If you itch your belly, it will get more stretch marks, and it will be difficult for you to get rid of these marks post-delivery.

Narrow Down Baby Names
Most parents always have a list of names that they like but it's not always necessary for partners to agree on the same names. Your second semester is a great time for you to narrow down names by involving the people you want to be a part of the process. The smartest thing to do would be to make a list of the names you and your partner like and share it with the people who you want suggestions

from. Select the most popular names and then being narrowing down the list on your own until you are left with a few names that you and your partner are both happy with.

Decide Whether You Want to Know the Sex of Your Baby

During the second trimester, you'll be able to ask your doctor whether you are having a girl or a boy. Knowing the gender is a personal choice. While some parents opt to learn the gender of the baby during delivery, they are others who want to know the sex of a baby before the baby arrives. If you want to have a gender reveal and you do not want to know the sex of the baby before the gender reveal, you can always ask your midwife to hand over the information to the person who is in charge of planning the gender reveal.

Note Down Your Pregnancy Dreams

When you are dreaming, there will be a lot of excitement with regards to the arrival of your baby. These happy thoughts are always healthy for you, and they help you stay in a positive place. It's important for you to note down all these dreams you have so that every time you feel low or unhappy, you can go through the journal and this will lift your spirits almost instantly.

Childbirth Classes

A lot of moms to me wonder why they need to sign up for childbirth class when they are in the second trimester. Believe me when I say this, these classes fill up so fast you may be left with no option but to go into labor without getting involved in the class if you don't sign up during your second trimester. Hospitals offer childbirth classes as well, but you can also choose a specialized childbirth session with your partner. Some parents also choose to have their babies delivered at home and if that is something you are looking to do, educate yourself as much as possible. One-on-one sessions are always recommended because you can have your partner with you and your healthcare provider can give you all the information you need with personal attention to ensure you are covered up.

Financial Planning

There are several responsibilities you must take up when you become a parent, and this includes educational expenses, healthcare, and a good lifestyle which requires savings. Make sure that you plan the expenses for your child in advance so that you can provide a secure environment and give your child a beautiful life.

Prepare Your Pets

It is important for you to keep your pets prepared about your pregnancy and the arrival of your baby because they need to learn and respect and care for the child. Instead of pondering about how you want to keep your baby away from the pet, try to create an environment where your pet and your baby get close to each other. You also need to decide for your pet during delivery, so you know someone is caring for your pet when you are in the hospital.

Start Child Care Research

There are various things you need to stay prepared for, and childcare is one of the most essential of them. If you plan on getting back to work after a few months of maternity leave, you need to get the best options for daycare or nanny care depending on what you think will be most feasible for your baby. You could also check and see if it will be possible for you to leave your baby with relatives or parents because this is a safer option.

Teeth Cleaning

That a lot of misconceptions regarding teeth cleaning during pregnancy. Not only is teach cleaning healthy but doing it during pregnancy is also something that is recommended by doctors. When you clean your teeth, you are less likely to transmit cavities and bacteria to your babies. The second trimester is a great time to get your teeth cleaned. When you go for a teeth cleaning session, make sure to inform your dentist about the pregnancy in case it's not obvious.

Celebrate Your Halfway Milestone

It important to celebrate every milestone in your life and 20 weeks is your halfway to pregnancy which is a moment worth celebrating. Indulge in a pedicure or a beautiful massage that soothes your senses. This is a great time to purchase maternity clothes and show off your baby bump with pride.

Sleeping on Your Side

While I already recommended this in the first trimester, you may want to start paying a little more attention to sleeping on your side in your second semester to help with the blood flow to your baby and reduce the swelling. This is where a pregnancy pillow comes in handy because you can slip it between your legs, and it comforts you and helps you sleep better.

Kegels Exercises

While I've done it all my life, you must start doing it during your second semester to help strengthen your muscles and prevent urine leaks which is common during pregnancy. Exercises also help to tone down your vagina, and this has sex more enjoyable for partners.

Baby Registry

Carrying a baby registry is practical, and if you are planning on having a baby shower, this is the first thing you should do. Make a list of everything you need and list it on the registry. While people don't have to buy all of it for you, you have at least half of the list covered up after the baby shower, and this will take off a huge burden from your shoulders. It also ensures that you don't get unnecessary gifts that you will not use.

Talk About Maternity Leave

If you are you working woman and career is important to you, now is the time for you to discuss your maternity leave, keeping in mind circumstances which could include bed rest, premature delivery or complications that could delay or prepone your maternity leave. Try delegating all your work or finishing up as much as possible before you sign off and decide which coworkers will handle your work in your absence.

Check Your Rings and Bracelets

If you wear earrings and bracelets, it is important for you to constantly keep checking if they have become tighter, because your body tends to swell up during pregnancy and if you are wearing jewelry that's too tight it could become uncomfortable. If you don't want to take off your wedding ring, just put it on the chain that will be very close to your heart.

Plan A Baby Shower

While the gift registry is part of a baby shower, it's not all you have to think about. Check for different ideas for the baby shower and let people know what you are looking forward to. While you may not have to plan your own baby shower, you can give people an idea of what you would like for your baby shower, so they know how to plan it.

Avoid Unsafe Activities

If you ride a bike or scooter, you may have to stop during your second trimester because there is a high risk of falling and this could cause trauma to your abdomen. You also need to stop any contact sports or something that involves too many jerks that could affect your baby.

Amusement park rides are also something you must stay away from, and scuba diving is something you must cross off the list.

Write A Letter to Your Baby

It's always beautiful to share your pregnancy experience with your child, and there's nothing better than writing down what your experience is all about as well as your hopes and dreams for your baby while your baby is still in your belly. Make a memento box and keep whatever you think will hold value and will be a cherished memory for your baby when he or she grows up. This memento box could later be gifted to your baby and will be a beautiful procession to have.

Home Improvement

Your second semester is a great time for you to start planning a nursery and space for your baby. If there are any new things you want to bring in, it should be done around this time, and any dangerous or hazardous areas should be fixed almost instantly. You should plan home improvement but try not to be a part of it because exposure to chemicals is not healthy for your baby. As much as you want, you cannot paint because going up a ladder is a complete no-no.

Things to Do During All Your Trimesters (Especially During the Second Trimester)

Pregnancy can be a stressful as well as an enjoyable phase in your life, and you need to make sure that you project the right mindset. The only way you will be able to make sure that you enjoy pregnancy is if you do things right and you keep you and your baby healthy. Here are a few things that you need to do during every trimester to ensure that you and your baby have a wonderful pregnancy.

Drink Lots of Water

Water is essential during your pregnancy, and you need to drink about 8 to 10 classes per day. If you are involved in any kind of physical activity or light training, then you need to add a little extra water to your daily diet. If you think that you are drinking less water than other women, do not worry. Some women need more water than you, and there is a possibility that you may end up drinking more than ten glasses of water daily. The best way to check whether you need water is by checking the color of your urine. If your urine is cloudy or dark yellow in color, then you need to make sure that you drink more water than you currently are. If your urine is pale yellow or clear, then you are drinking the perfect amount of water.

Stretching

While stretching is easier to do in the first trimester, it gets difficult from the second trimester onwards because of the growth of your baby bump. Rather than sitting around and feeling lethargic, you need to make sure that you continue stretching your muscles so that it does not tighten up. When your muscles are losing you will feel a lot more relaxed, and your flexibility will also be enhanced. This proves to be extremely crucial when you go into labor.

Pregnancy Power Naps

While it is important to stay active and keep your muscles loose, you also need to reward yourself with a few power naps through the day. Taking a quick 15-minute nap will make sure that you are energized through the rest of the day and you will be able to get rid of the fatigue that you may be facing. If you are at your workplace, then you can go to the nearest conference room or even close the door to your office and take a quick power nap. Whatever you do, you need to make sure that you have set an alarm on your phone so that you do not oversleep as you may not feel that great after sleeping for long hours in the middle of the day.

Healthy Snacks

One thing that you should be aware of is your hunger pangs will keep getting worse in your second trimester. Since your baby is growing, you will feel a lot hungrier, and you will need to snack every couple of hours. Rather than binge eating unhealthy snacks, you need to make sure that you keep your nutritional snacks ready everywhere you are because hunger can strike anywhere. If your morning sickness has not cleared even during your second trimester, then you can keep your trusted crackers available to eat whenever you feel hungry.

Relax as Much as Possible

Relaxing is very underrated during pregnancy, and you need to make sure that you give your body enough rest and relaxation irrespective of your schedule for the day. Some of the better techniques to employ are prenatal yoga, deep breathing along with progressive muscle relaxation. These exercises will ensure that you sleep better, and you will feel completely relaxed.

Power Walks

I've already touched on the fact that power walks can be dangerous if your belly size is too big. Different women have different belly sizes during the second trimester. If your belly size is not that big and you are comfortable walking, then you can do so provided there is someone along with you. If you are not confident about walking quickly, then you need to avoid it because it could be dangerous for you as well as your baby.

Pregnancy Superfoods

I have already covered all the foods that need to be eaten during your pregnancy. However, your second trimester is extremely crucial, and you need to munch as many superfoods as possible during this phase. Some of the foods include veggies, fruits, yogurt, Salmon, Walnuts, eggs, sweet potatoes and beans. Eating these superfoods at least four or five times a day will make sure that you are extremely healthy, and your baby will grow at a very normal pace.

Start Maintaining A Journal

Pregnancy is an exciting phase in every woman's life, and you may want to share these memories with your child at some point in time. Maintaining a journal and making notes will not any help lift your spirits; it will also make sure that your child appreciates all that you've done to give him or her a healthy life. You will also be able to make sure that you see what triggers your illnesses and what foods you are allergic to. Maintaining a journal during the second trimester is crucial not only from a mental perspective but also from your health perspective.

Weight Gain

By the time you reach your second trimester, you will know what your healthy weight range is and at what pace you are gaining weight. Keeping track of your weight and the progress will ensure that you are taking all the precautionary steps in case something is not right. You should also try not to panic if you do not see too much growth happening in the first couple of weeks of the second trimester. Always stay in touch with your doctor and make sure that he monitors your situation perfectly in order to avoid any unfortunate circumstances.

Do Nice Things

If you are at home and you do not feel too good, there is no harm in heading out to get a pedicure done or to watch a movie. When you do things that you love, you will start enjoying your pregnancy, and this will put you in the perfect frame of mind. Try surprising your partner with a romantic dinner and show him that you appreciate all the support that he is providing you. When you take a break from the stress of pregnancy you will feel relaxed and in a happier state of mind.

Check with Your Friends

That may be times that you come across certain scenarios that you are not sure about and in such situations, it is best to check with a friend that has been through the journey of pregnancy. A friend will be very frank with her experiences, and she will let you know exactly what to expect and what her fears were. While your husband may be away for work for most of the day, you need to make sure that you have someone by your side and a friend can help you in this regard.

Identify Problems

You need to make sure that you identify any problems that you will be facing during your pregnancy and the second trimester is the ideal time to find out these problems and tackle them. Here are a few problems that you need to look out for and contact your doctor immediately:

- If your baby is kicking around lesser than usual or not moving around as much as he or she used to.

- Vaginal spotting or bleeding.

- Vaginal discharge changing from a milky white to bloody or watery.

- After 37 weeks of pregnancy, your mucus discharge should increase. Contact your doctor if this does not happen.

Mindful Pregnancy for New Moms

- Increased pelvic pressure.

- Severe lower back pain (especially if it was not happening during the first trimester).

- Stomach pain or menstrual cramping.

- Experiencing more than six contractions in an hour before your 37 weeks is up.

- Painful burning sensation while urinating.

- During the urge to urinate even after you're gone a couple of minutes back.

- No urination or little urination.

- Blood tinged or cloudy urination.

- Sudden chills or experiencing of your higher than 100.4 degrees Fahrenheit.

- Sudden vomiting accompanied by fever or pain.

- Visual problems such as blurring, double vision, flashing lights, dimming or spots in your line of vision. These are all probable symptoms of preeclampsia.

- Puffiness around your eyes or swelling in your face.

- More than normal weight gain.

- Any kind of abdominal injury due to a fall or a minor accident.

- Persistent itching of your arms, torso, legs, soles or palms.

- Pain in your shoulder or upper belly.

- Flu-like symptoms such as cough, sore throat, sudden fever, stuffy or runny nose, body aches, exertion or sudden chills.

- Frequent vomiting or diarrhea.

- Profound feelings of sadness or hopelessness can lead to panic attacks or depression or even anxiety.

- Any of your current health problems getting worse such as worsening asthma.

Take Photos of Your Belly

Parents love documenting the progress during pregnancy and taking photos of your belly is a great way to do that. Not only will you be able to monitor the progress, but you will also be able to collect a lot of memories and share them with your child at some point in their life.

Chapter 9:
Third Trimester Essential Secrets

The third trimester is the final stage before your baby arrives. This trimester should be focused completely upon preparing for the arrival of your baby and making sure you are as prepared as you can be to go into labor. Here is what you need to do to prepare effectively for your third trimester.

Beware of Your Baby's Movements

Your baby is going to move around in your belly a lot during the third trimester, and you will figure out a pattern in the movement of your child within a few weeks. Your baby will also sleep, so you will figure out when your baby is resting and when your baby is awake. You will also realize when your baby is moving towards labor, and this is the time you need to contact your midwife or doctor immediately.

Learn About Third Trimester Antenatal Appointments

This is the final step of appointments you must go through prior to going into labor, and this always includes preparation for labor and birth as well as understanding how you can recognize the signs of labor and deal with labor pains when they happen. This is around the time you will realize how big your bump has grown and you can check your baby's growth depending on the measurements. You can also go for an ultrasound during your third trimester, and this is going to give you a full view of your baby.

Most first-time mums need to go through something that is known as a membrane sweep during the 40th week. This usually helps induce labor, and in case it doesn't, you must go through another one during your 41st week. Women who are having a baby for the second time usually go through this sweep in the 41st week.

Be Cautious About Pregnancy Signs You Shouldn't Ignore

Your third trimester is probably one of those times where you believe you are going to face a lot of pains and cramping which is why you try to look for some warning signs. If you know that your baby isn't moving as much, it's important for you to call the doctor immediately and let them know that something isn't right. While your midwife will ensure that she gets everything covered for you in all the tests to keep your pregnancy healthy, you need to always look out for signs such as you are feeling your blood pressure is a little high or you are suffering from a severe headache or blurred vision. Nausea and vomiting are also signing you shouldn't ignore during the third trimester.

Eat Well

This is something you must do throughout your pregnancy, and I say it again, during the third trimester you must stay healthy and include as much iron rich food as possible to help form the red blood cells in your baby. A lot of lean meats and green leafy vegetables are highly recommended, and you can always wash it down with a big glass of orange juice to help your body absorb the iron more effectively.

Start Stretching

You need to loosen up your body for birth, so stretching is recommended because it helps to release the body from the pain of contractions and prevents cramping, especially in the legs during the time of labor. Just move around slowly and stretch gently to keep your muscles relaxed and ensure that there is no cramping.

Massage Your Bump

Massaging your bump has plenty of benefits. It helps you connect with your baby, and it also increases closeness when you feel your little baby kick. Encourage your partner to rub your belly with gentle strokes to increase the connection and always wait to do this when you know your baby is going to be most active. When you feel your baby kick inside of you, it brings you a lot of joy, and it makes the entire experience worthwhile.

Put Together Furniture and Buy A Stroller

When you have the nursery or your baby space set up, make sure to purchase the right furniture for your baby. Don't spend on too many items because these aren't going to be used forever. You should instead focus on the ones that are essential. A bassinet and a stroller are highly recommended because you will need both items for a while after the baby arrives, and it will make life easier. The reason it is good to put up the bassinet and purchase a stroller now is that you will not need to stress about it once the baby arrives.

Talk to Your Baby

Even your partner should spend a lot of time talking to your baby because your baby can hear voices and start recognizing them from the womb itself. Listening to soothing music and reading a book or a magazine to your baby is something that will make your baby feel connected with you. You can also sing to your baby and make your baby feel happy. It is also important for you to stay calm and composed during the last trimester because the more you stress, the more your baby senses it, and it increases insecurity. Create a happy atmosphere around you if you want your baby to be healthy.

Identify the Signs Of labor As Well As the Stages

It's not easy to predict when labor will strike or how long it is going to last but understanding the procedure can help you control the situation and feel more relaxed. There is a total of three stages of labor which include the contractions, the actual delivery, and the placenta. Make sure to cover up all these three stages, so you have information about what lies ahead and how you must deal with it.

Birth Plan

The third trimester is the perfect time for you to discuss the birth plan and see how you want your baby to be delivered. Whether are you looking for a vaginal delivery or a C-section, it's always better to be prepared for both because sometimes women who want to go for a vaginal delivery may not be able to because of certain complications and they may have to head in for a C-section. Being prepared for both kinds of labor just helps you relax during the process irrespective.

Contraction

The first time that you start getting labor contractions, it is going to begin very gently and eventually escalate into the real labor pain. It begins with the muscles in your worm starting to tighten from time to time. Almost all women go through this pain while some may just go into labor without any contractions whatsoever. The interval between each contraction is what determines how soon you are going to deliver so it is important for you to keep track. Contractions usually occur at regular intervals, so it is important for you to notice how far apart they are because this will determine how long it is before you get into labor. It's important for you to also learn how to deal with contractions because stressing during this time could make it more difficult for you to deliver a baby. The best way to deal with contractions is to have your partner by your side and guide you through the process. You can try practicing this in advance so that you do not have to stress when it happens.

Buy Clothes for The Baby

If you haven't gotten all the essentials that you need for your baby through the gift registry, make sure to purchase everything else that's needed well in advance. If you were given these clothes as a gift during your baby shower, you need to make sure that you wash them with non-biological washing powder and keep them ready for your baby to wear.

Pack Your Hospital Bag

It's important for you to make sure you get your hospital bag ready and add everything inside it so that you don't stress out during your stay at the hospital. I will discuss all the essential items you need to pack in your hospital bag in Chapter 11 so you can take notes.

Sleep

I can't stress on this enough but trust me when I say sleep! These are the last few months that you can relax before you go into labor and then there are going to be a few months of sleepless nights. So, you need to rest as much as possible during pregnancy so that you have the energy to look after your baby. When you sleep, it helps to relax your body, and it also keeps your baby calm. It's important for you to sleep on your side because this reduces the risk of stillbirth and it helps your baby's blood flow to be constant.

Household Supplies

Your baby is approaching soon, and you will need to make sure that you make your life a lot easier right now because there could be a lot of your time taken up with the baby. You need to start stocking up on your household supplies and purchase things that your family may need when you are not able to take care of them post-delivery. These include tinned foods, cleaning products or even frozen vegetables. The reason you need to do this is because shopping will become a huge task and you need to give all the attention to your baby when he or she does arrive. You should also try and cook up a few portions that you can freeze ahead of your first few weeks of being a new parent. This will take away the stress of having to cook while your baby is in your arms.

Baby Car Seat

Most women have a baby in a hospital and going home by car can be quite difficult for the baby as well as the mother. You need to make sure that you keep the baby as comfortable as possible and installing a baby car seat will help you as well as your baby sit comfortably while going back home. You get various car seats depending on your baby's weight. You need to pick the right one and get it installed by professionals so that it is fitted properly. Never buy one because it looks good. It needs to fit your car perfectly, and the belt should fasten without too much problem.

Third Trimester Sex

If your pregnancy is not filled with complications and you and your baby are healthy, you can continue having sex right until you go into labor. You will need to speak with your doctor with regards to the positions that you can have sex in because the pump will keep getting bigger as the days go by. You need to think of your comfort level along with your baby's comfort level.

Get as Much Help as Possible

Do not be afraid to ask for favors because friends and family members will always be there to help. Feeling guilty is not going to help you because your friends and family members are just waiting for you to ask and they will be ready to help in any way possible. Make the most of these helpers and get them to tidy up the house or even help when the baby comes back home. It is always better to have women around that have undergone pregnancy as they will be able to give you better advice and take care of you in a much better manner.

Check the Hospital

If you have decided to have a baby in a hospital, then you need to make sure that you take a tour of the hospital. You can also check the route that you will take to get to the hospital so that you do not get stuck in traffic. You also need to make sure that you check the hospital's policies with regards to insurance and book your room as soon as possible so that you are staying in comfort.

Keep Your Back Healthy

Your back is very crucial during the third trimester as you head into labor. You need to keep it as healthy as possible, and if your bump is giving you any kind of aches in your back, then you need to make sure that you try to avoid any heavy lifting or putting any strain on your back. If the pain is too much, you can even speak to your physiotherapist and get a maternity belt that will help support your back.

Prepare Well

You need to make sure that you and your partner are synced with regards to the childbirth and you have everything in order. You need to have your midwife's number as well as your doctor's number available. If you have other children or pets, then you need to arrange for someone to come and take care of them when you and your partner move to the hospital for delivery. If your children or your pets are alone at home while you are in delivery, it may put additional stress on you, and this is not good for you or the baby.

Hypnobirthing

Hypnobirthing is the latest trend that is catching up these days, and you can speak to your doctor regarding the hypnobirthing techniques. These are nothing but visualization as well as breathing techniques that will help you stay extremely calm and in complete control when you are giving birth.

Read as Much as Possible

If you been reading about pregnancy for the first two trimesters, then you need to start reading about babies in the third trimester. You need to read as much as possible regarding baby care because you will not have time to read once your baby is here. You need to see how the first few weeks will change your life and what you can do to ease your stress.

Breastfeeding
You need to start preparing for breastfeeding and understand how it works as well as realize its benefits. While breastfeeding is natural for some women, it can get complicated for others, and you need to make sure that you are successful at it. You may want to attend a breastfeeding class when you are pregnant, and this will help you prepare in the right manner.

Natural labor
These days it is very common for doctors to induce labor because they are not sure what causes natural labor to start. If you feel that you are overdue, and you are not going into labor, you may want to try some of the various things that can bring about natural labor. These include having sex, walking, eating curry or even acupuncture.

Baby Development
The third trimester is extremely crucial for your baby, and you need to make sure that you follow your baby's development as closely as possible. Tracking the development on a weekly basis will help you feel relaxed and take preventive measures whenever necessary. The closer you get to your delivery, the better it is that you stay prepared for any complications. Tracking your baby's development is the best

way to stay in control of your pregnancy and taking care of your child in the right manner.

Chapter 10:
Prevent Stretch Marks Hacks

Stretch marks are common, and 90% of women get them during the sixth or the seventh month of pregnancy. Stretch marks make your skin look bad, and women try to do whatever it is in their power to keep them away. While there is no proven method for you to keep stretch marks away or avoid them completely, there are a few hacks that you could try to reduce the marks, depending on your skin type. I know several women who have gone through pregnancy, but some of them have stretch marks on the stomach while others have a stomach that is smooth. While I did care if there were stretch marks on my stomach, they weren't as bad as some of my friends. It is healthy to accept your scars because it reminds you of what you've been through. This doesn't mean you can't try to keep them away. Here are a few things about stretch marks that I figured out based on my friends and their pregnancy.

- Stretch marks are genetic. A lot of my friends had mothers that complained about them having similar marks on their belly.

- Women who gain more weight during pregnancy get more stretch marks.

- Dark skinned moms are less likely to get stretch marks in comparison to the others.

Stretch marks are basically tiny tears that occur in the layer of tissue under your skin because it's pulled to its limit during pregnancy. While it can't be avoided completely here is what you can do to try and reduce the risk of stretch marks during pregnancy.

Eating Right

It's necessary for you to eat right during pregnancy. Apart from help with the development of your baby, a lot of people don't know that the right food can also help control stretch marks on your stomach. This is because when you have enough vitamins and nutrients in your body, it benefits your skin and enhances the elasticity which limits the risk of a stretch mark from occurring. Foods that are rich in antioxidants can help keep your skin strong and flexible. Include berries and a lot of spinach in your diet if you want to limit the risk of stretch marks. Vitamin E protects the membranes of your skin cells which limit stretch marks, and therefore you need to consume a lot of avocados and greens. Vitamin A helps with skin tissue repair so vegetables like carrot, sweet potatoes, bell peppers, and squash work wonders. Omega 3 keeps cell membranes healthy and helps your skin get a beautiful glow as well as moisturizers it. Foods like fish and fish oil are great.

Exercising

Exercising helps to retain the elasticity of your skin, and this also enhances circulation which makes sure you don't put on too much weight. It's the weight gain at an accelerated rate that is one of the leading causes of stretch marks, and when you gain healthy weight during your pregnancy, you automatically limit the risk of getting stretch marks.

Watch Your Weight

Women believe they need to put on a lot of weight during pregnancy and this is a big misconception. While you do need to have a certain amount of weight gain to have a healthy pregnancy you don't have to gain so much weight that you end up being obese because this will simply increase stretch marks, and it will make you unhealthy. The key to staying healthy during your pregnancy is to eat smaller meals at regular intervals and eat healthy food rather than unhealthily, and weight gaining food items.

Staying Hydrated

Drinking lots of water does not only take care of your health as well as your baby's health, but it also provides several other benefits. Water is a great source of detoxification and it also helps your skin cope with all the stretching. When you drink a gallon of water daily, you will improve the elasticity of your skin and all the toxins from your body will be eliminated. You should also try and include food that has a high-water content as this will help you stay hydrated throughout the day. When your skin stays hydrated, there will be no stretch marks that will appear because the hydration helps the elasticity of the skin. Including foods such as strawberries, watermelons and cucumbers will help your skin stretch very easily and will keep stretch marks away.

Avoid Chemicals

There are several body washes that are said to contain harsh chemicals. These chemicals not only dry your skin, but it will also affect the elasticity of the skin over a period. You need to start looking for body washes and cleansers that are made using natural oils. These natural oils will help hydrate your skin, and it will make it a lot more elastic. If you are not sure which cleanser you should purchase, then you can also use coconut oil as a skin cleanser. All you need to do is rub it all over your skin and then rinse the oil off with warm water. When you do this, you need to pat yourself dry using a soft towel, and your skin will feel refreshed in no time.

Using Supplements

A lot of people lose the elasticity of their skin as they grow older, and once this happens to your skin, it can never return to the size that it was. Often it is the diet that you eat that also contributes towards your skin losing its elasticity. If your diet does not give you proper nutrients as well as vitamins, then you need to take a few supplements that will help improve the elasticity of your skin. Some of the supplements that you should opt-in for are:

- Vitamin C supplements that are essential for producing elastin as well as collagen.

- Vitamin E supplements that will purify your skin and work as an antioxidant.

- Vitamin D supplements that help with the creation of new growth cells in the body.

Massage Your Tummy

You no longer need to purchase any expensive creams that promise to keep away stretch marks. These creams do not achieve anything, and they are not going to keep stretch marks away that easily. One of the benefits of investing in these creams is it helps to moisturize your belly and it will keep away the dryness as well as itchy skin. When you are pregnant you will need to take care of stretch marks around your tummy, your lower back, your legs as well as your thighs. These are the parts of your body that undergo a lot of strain when your baby is growing inside you. The skin around these areas will keep on itching; however, you need to make sure that you keep the skin moisturized in order to prevent any marks from forming.

Mindful Pregnancy for New Moms

Avoid investing in ordinary moisturizers because they will not be able to penetrate the skin properly. You need to make sure that you invest in a lotion that will help penetrate your skin and prevent any marks from forming. You need to apply this lotion on your most prone areas at least twice a day. Some of the lotions that you invest in should contain collagen, cocoa butter, shea butter, and elastin. These elements help the elasticity of the skin. You can also look for a firming butter that has Vitamin E as well as ginseng in it. These elements help to rejuvenate the skin and soften it. Whichever lotion you invest in, you need to make sure that you massage your belly properly after applying it because this will help the lotion penetrate and give relief and keep away the stretch marks.

Chapter 11:
Necessity Bag Items to Bring for Labor

Going into labor is quite stressful and heading to the hospital is the first thing that comes to your mind the minute you hear the word contractions. There is a reason why I mentioned you should keep your hospital bag ready to just pick up and leave when you head out to the hospital but what you need to put inside the bag is also crucial. The sooner you start packing your bag, the less likely it is that you will miss out on anything. The best way to ensure you have everything covered is to make a list and take off everything that is added to the bag. Here is a list that I prepared for myself and found extremely helpful.

Hospital Id and Paperwork
You need to make sure you carry the hospital identification proof that is needed as well as any other documentation including insurance, if you have it covered for your maternity. Try making a few copies and create a file that you slip into your hospital bag. Make sure you neatly arrange all the documents and keep copies available to pull out easily when needed. Ask the hospital are the documents you and your partner need to carry and keep those ready in the bag as well.

Birth Plan

If you have a good plan ready, make sure to print it out on a paper and get a few copies of it handed out to the doctors in case that is something you want them to understand in specific, and you are in too much pain to discuss. Inform your partner about this copy and make sure that your partner keeps them ready when the time arrives.

Bathrobe

It's important for you to have a soft bathrobe ready with you because this is the most comfortable attire you can wear when you are in labor. It's also convenient to slip back into the robe post-delivery when you are recovering. Some hospitals allow you to wear whatever you are comfortable in during delivery and I chose to wear a bathrobe because it was so convenient and comfortable.

Socks

The labor room usually has the AC at a very low temperature so you may tend to get cold feet - literally! A good pair of socks can keep your feet warm during labor.

Slippers or Flip Flops

You will need a nice comfortable pair of slippers or flip flops that you will need to wear when you walk around the hospital for the delivery as well as afterward. Do not opt-in for shoes that you need to struggle to get into or something that requires bending because this will be too much of a hassle.

Lip Balm

Your lips will dry out when you visit the hospital, especially during labor so keeping a lip balm by your side can help you feel comfortable and hydrate your lips.

Body Lotion or Massage Oil

When you are stressed the best thing to do is get yourself a massage or ask your partner to do it for you, and in this situation, body lotion and massage oil can come in handy.

Water Spray or Sponge

If you start feeling hot during labor using a water spray around your face and neck or keeping a sponge on your forehead can help cool you down. Inform your partner with regards to what needs to be done in this situation and how to keep the water spray or sponge ready.

Entertainment

For some people labors are quick, but for others, it could go on for days so always prepare yourself for the worst and go prepared. You will most likely spend a few hours before you are in labor and the best way to keep calm is to entertain yourself by reading a book or a magazine on even listening to some soothing music.

Eye Mask and Ear Plugs

It is good to keep an eye mask and ear plugs ready when you require to rest. This will keep away any interruptions.

Night Gowns

While the bathrobe can help you during labor, you need something to stay comfortable for the days that you may spend in the hospital and a loose nightgown is the perfect choice. You may want to shop for a night gown and choose a front opening one that can make it convenient for you to breastfeed.

Maternity Pads

Your hospital will provide you with these, but it is always necessary to pack an extra box just in case. Maternity pads are bigger and softer in comparison to normal sanitary napkins. They are used after your delivery or even at times when you need something that is super absorbent. You will need to wear one post-delivery and you may have to change your pad every one or two hours post-delivery so purchasing your own box of Maternity pads will help you through these hours.

Underwear

Make sure that you pack many pairs of comfortable and large underwear that can accommodate the heavy-duty maternity pads you need to use for a few days.

Bras

Get your hands-on nursing bras that are made of cotton and will not hurt you. I had spoken about this in chapter 1, and I repeat this again, always look for cotton and soft nursing bras because when you start breastfeeding, it could be a little uncomfortable, and your body will take a while to adjust to lactation and breastfeeding.

Toiletries
Pack a lot of tissues, your hairbrush, your comb, your deodorant, toothpaste and toothbrush, shampoo, hair conditioner, hair clips, and hair ties and spare plastic bags to keep dirty clothes in.

Cosmetics
If you like wearing makeup on a regular basis carry just the basic like your lip liner, lipstick, eyeliner, and moisturizer. Don't forget sunscreen for when you leave the hospital.

Glasses or Contact Lenses
If you are carrying magazines and books to read, you will need your glasses so don't forget to pack them.

Phone and Charger
It's really important for you to stay in touch with your loved ones when you are in the hospital and the best way to do it is with your phone so make sure to pack your charger and your phone, so you can use it.

Clothes
You need a clean pair of complete clothes to wear when you leave the hospital so pack something that you know is easy to slip on and will keep you comfortable on your journey home.

Snacks and Drinks

Labor could be long sometimes, and if you feel hungry in between, you can always have a quick snack or a drink to sip on. Remember to pack your favorite snacks because you may start craving for this once you've delivered.

Packing Hospital Bag for Your Partner

Your partner is also extremely crucial to the process of delivery, and he will also need a hospital bag to help him function in a better manner. Here are a few hospital bag essentials for your partner.

Snacks Along with Water

Labor can be a very stressful situation for you as well as your partner. You should always consider packing in a few snacks along with a couple of water bottles for your partner in his hospital bag. Also, make sure that you pack as much change as possible for the hospital vending machine.

Gadgets and Chargers

Gadgets such as cell phones, cameras, and video cameras are essential when you are capturing something as beautiful as childbirth. Your partner will need a phone to stay in touch with the other family members and friends that could not make it to the hospital. He will also need the camera as well as a video camera to capture all the memories and click some happy pictures once the baby has arrived. These pictures are memories for a lifetime, and this is something that your partner needs to do in order to look back fondly on these memories later.

Clothes

Your partner should always carry an extra set of clothes because labor could be ongoing for long hours, and in some cases even days. You need to make sure that he is always comfortable, and this is where a change of clothes will come in handy.

Toiletries

Toiletries are essential for your partner when you are in labor or post-delivery as well. Most hospitals allow the partner to freshen up in the hospital shower and if that is the case, you may want your partner to carry along his body wash as well as a personal towel.

Spare Lenses

If your partner wears, contact lenses then you may want to make sure that he carries an extra pair as this could come in handy. As I said, it can be a long day in labor, and this could put a lot of stress on your partner.

Inflatable Pillow

Asking your partner to pack his own pillow may not be very feasible, and this is where an inflatable pillow can come in handy. This will allow your partner to catch a few winks every now and then if the labor process is getting too stressful.

Entertainment Options

Carrying a few things to stay entertained can be useful. Some of these things should be a tablet or even the latest book or maybe a music player that you can plug in and listen to your favorite songs. You and your partner need to do everything possible in order to relieve the stress and entertainment is the best way to take your mind off all the physical and mental strain that you will be going through.

Packing Hospital Bag for Your Baby

While you may pack a hospital bag for you and your partner you should not forget the needs of your baby. Your baby will need a few things when he or she arrives and keeping a hospital bag ready for your baby is an extremely smart thing to do. Here are a few essentials in your baby's hospital bag that you should not forget about:

Bodysuits

Most hospitals will usually provide your baby with a few clothes to wear. Some hospitals would even have policies with regards to what the baby can and cannot wear post birth. You may want to check with the hospital and carry a few extra layers of clothing in case you feel that the temperature is too cold. Always opt-in for bodysuits that can be fastened upfront so that it will be comfortable to put on for the baby and you will not have to worry about hurting the baby as well.

Booties and Socks

It is essential to keep your newborn baby warm all the time, and this is where booties and socks come in handy. You may also want to carry a hat for your baby if you feel that the lighting in the hospital room is too bright. This will also help for the first few weeks after birth.

Homecoming Outfit

Your baby coming home for the first time is a very important milestone, and you need to make sure that the baby is very comfortable and looks good at the same time. You also need to consider weather conditions and see what will suit your baby the best. If the weather outside is warm, you can consider dressing the baby in a bodysuit along with hat and booties. If the weather is too cold, then you will want to carry a jacket or a snowsuit along with mittens for your baby. You need to remember that your baby will not be able to tell you if he or she is comfortable or not. You need to recognize the baby's condition and make sure that you are making the right decision on their behalf.

Blankets

Most hospitals will usually provide plenty of blankets in order to keep the mother and the baby warm post birth. However, carrying your own blanket is essential because this will be helpful when you are taking your baby back in the car where you will need to wrap up the baby. A blanket is also helpful when relatives and friends come to visit the baby, and they may want to carry the baby. A blanket is a great way to avoid skin to skin contact with other people because the baby may not like everyone's touch. Here are a few more essentials that you need to do when you arrive with your partner at the hospital.

Speak to The Staff

When you arrive at the hospital, you need to make sure that you speak with the hospital staff and make the ambiance as amiable as possible. You can ask the staff to lower the lighting or even have special food arrangements done if you are allergic to something. While it is advisable to carry your own food, there is always the possibility of you running out of food, and this is where you need to make the hospital staff aware of your allergies and your diet.

Accommodations

You also need to look at hospital accommodations and make sure that you have a private room along with a private bathroom. You also need to make sure that your room is big enough to accommodate your partner for the night and there is enough room for you to walk around while you are preparing for labor.

Chapter 12:
Essential Recovery Secrets After Birth

Childbirth is not easy irrespective of what method of delivery you have chosen. Once your baby enters the world, it's a lot of excitement and happiness, but it's also the period of your recovery. Once your baby is into the world, you now need to give your body enough time to relax because it needs to adjust to the various changes.

There is no fixed time for how long your body is going to take to recover because different women required a different amount of time to heal depending on the postpartum symptoms. Most of your problems ease away within a week, but others may take a longer time to heal. Sore nipples and backaches are common symptoms that may last longer.

Vaginal birth may seem like it is the easier route for most women, but you still need to rest your body in order to recover completely. Your perineum will take a few weeks to heal depending on if you had a perineal tear or an episiotomy. An episiotomy cut is one of the most painful cuts that you can experience but thankfully not a lot of women go through this nowadays. Always try to avoid the episiotomy cut as much as possible and don't use it unless necessary. This is usually a cut made from the perineal area right up to the rectum to make way for the baby's head to come out during a vaginal birth. A vaginal tear, on the other hand, is a tear that happens naturally when a woman's vagina starts to stretch for delivery. There are different kinds of vaginal tears and while the first degree of a vagina tear is only the first layer of skin, the second degree could include muscle rupturing as well which will take a longer time to heal.

A C-section will require even longer, and if you've been through a c-section, then you may want to consider spending an extra few days in the hospital to enhance the healing process. For your body to completely recover from a C-section, you need to rest a lot, but sometimes it could take a little longer. What's important is that you give your body enough time to heal and ensure that you do not stress too much post-delivery so that you recover completely.

Bleeding After Birth

Postpartum bleeding, which is also known as lochia, usually lasts about six weeks after delivery. It will be like a heavy period that takes out the leftover blood from your uterus along with all the other waste material that your body needs to discard. The first three to 10 days are usually very heavy, and this blood is the extra blood that is getting out of your system which will also include blood clots. You will need to change your pad once every 1 to 2 hours. You must rely on heavy-duty maternity pads which is why I highly suggest you carry a couple of them on your way to the hospital. Women that are used to tampons need to stay off them during the healing process because you will be too sensitive to insert a tampon.

Postpartum Depression

Most women believe that they will not suffer from postpartum depression because of the excitement and joy of having a baby, the truth is postpartum depression happens for most women, and they tend to feel hopeless, isolated, irritable, anxious and sad during this time. With all the attention on your baby, you are bound to feel left out, and this will increase the depression. Postpartum depression affects about one in three new moms, and you need to understand that the sooner you accept you are feeling depressed, the sooner you will be able to get help. You need to recover quickly because this will not only affect your baby, but it will also affect your own health. Postpartum depression could be overwhelming but when you don't deal with it effectively not only will you overcome it, but you will actually start enjoying the true meaning of motherhood, and you will manage to accept the changes that have occurred in your life.

Postpartum Healing

Healing postpartum is essential, and there are several steps that you need to keep in mind to make the healing process faster. Keep the steps in mind to make your postpartum healing a lot quicker.

Perineum Healing

You need to make sure that you give your perineum enough time to recover and you need to apply ice every couple of hours once you have given birth. You need to also make sure that you spray enough warm water over the area before you urinate and even after. This will make sure that the urine does not irritate the torn skin. You can also try taking warm baths for about 20 minutes more than a couple of times a day. This will help to ease the pain and accelerate the recovery process. You should also make sure that you do not sit or stand for long hours. Even when you are sleeping, you need to sleep on your side.

C-Section Scar
If you have had a C-section, then you need to make sure that you clean the c-section area gently at least once a day with soap and warm water. You need to then try the area with a clean towel and apply some sort of antibiotic ointment that your doctor may have suggested. You should also speak to your doctor if you need to leave the wound open or cover it up. Apart from carrying your baby, you should avoid carrying anything else and stay away from vigorous exercise until your doctor gives you the go ahead.

Try to Ease Your Aches and Pains
Once you have delivered your baby, there will be a lot of aching because of the amount of pushing that you have been doing. You can speak to your doctor to provide you with a painkiller or some sort of sedative that can help you forget the pain that you are going through.

You could also opt -in for a hot shower or use a heating pad that can help comfort the area where you are sore. Getting a light massage from your partner can also help take care of your aches and pains.

Regular Bowel Movement

The first bowel movement that you have post-delivery will take a lot of time, but you do not have to push it. You should consume a lot of food that is rich in fiber and try and go for walks daily. If all of this is still not helping, you can even use a gentle stool softener that will help you become regular. You should not push too much because your C-section scar may tear.

Kegels Exercises

In order to relieve your vagina from all the stress and bring it back in shape, you need to make sure that you do your Kegels regularly. You should make sure that you start your Kegels exercises as soon as you are comfortable and do three sets daily.

Aching Breasts

It is normal that your breasts will start aching once you have delivered because the process of breastfeeding must begin. In order to treat your sore breasts, you can start using ice packs or a warm heat pad that will help ease the aches. You can also check with your doctor in case you are suffering from cracked nipples or sore nipples.

Doctors Appointment

Once you have been discharged from the hospital and you reach home along with your baby you need to make sure that you keep up with your appointments with your doctor regularly. Apart from helping you physically cope with the stress of a C-section; your doctor will also help you cope with the emotional stress. The doctor also needs to check the wound and see if it is time to take out the stitches or if it needs to be left longer. You need to also inform your doctor if you are experiencing any kind of pain or occasional fever.

Ease Your Fatigue

Fatigue plays an important factor even post-delivery, and just like you did during your pregnancy, you need to make sure that you eat regularly throughout the day so that you will be able to recover from your fatigue and take care of your baby. Eat multiple small meals through the day rather than eating three large meals. Also, try and intake as many proteins and carbs as possible and drink a lot of water. Also keep in mind that just because you have delivered, it doesn't mean that you can consume caffeine or drink alcohol. Try and stay away from this as much as possible because it will affect your mood and it will make it very difficult for you to sleep.

Move Around

While exercises are off limits, you need to make sure that you move around a little bit as this will help you recover from your c-section a lot better. Some women even try and use a stroller to walk around as it helps with their pelvic movements and it also eases the pain. Do not overdo it if it is hurting too much or if you are bleeding. You may want to consult your doctor if moving around the house is extremely difficult.

Chapter 13:
Losing the Weight After Birth

You are expected to gain a certain amount of weight when you are pregnant, and a healthy amount is anywhere between 12 to 16 kgs. Some pregnant women, however, start gaining a lot more than that and while they do lose weight at the delivery table itself, it is important for you to follow a healthy lifestyle if you want to lose more of it. Most of the weight that you gain consists of your actual baby, the placenta, amniotic fluid and breast tissue that starts storing more fat.

If you have gained anywhere above 16 kg, then it's time for you to think about following a healthy diet if you want to shed your pregnancy weight. Most pregnant women tend to gain a lot of weight, and this increases the risk of them becoming overweight post pregnancy and increases the risk of diabetes and heart diseases. It also increases the risk in your future pregnancies. If you want to stay healthy here are a few ways you can get rid of excess weight once you deliver your baby.

Be Realistic

It's easy to look at pictures prior to pregnancy and wish you got back to the same size almost instantly. This is something that doesn't happen soon, and you got to give your body time to heal. It took nine months to get here and it will take you at least the same amount of time if not longer to get back to your pre-pregnancy figure. While this is not impossible to achieve, you must target what's important to make sure you give yourself a realistic time frame, so you don't disappoint yourself. You should try to lose about 1 kg or 2 kgs in a month and nothing more because anything higher than this means you are not losing weight in a healthy way and this will affect the growth and management of your baby's weight too.

Don't Crash Diet

This diet is not recommended for new moms because it doesn't focus on nutrient content. Your body will not be able to provide the right nourishment for your baby if you are breastfeeding. A crash diet simply means to cut down on your meals and eat very small proportions without taking into consideration the kind of nutrition you're providing to your body. While this diet worked when you were a teenager, it's not healthy for you to go on a crash diet when you're a mom because you need to keep yourself strong and nourished if you want to look after your baby and keep your baby healthy. You should plan effective long-term solutions to lose weight where your health is kept at a top priority. Opting in for weight loss diets that do not provide your body with effective nutrition will decrease the amount of breast milk your body forms and your baby will be left hungry and malnourished.

Breastfeed If You Can

Nowadays several doctors recommend formula milk because women want to get back to work as soon as possible and it's difficult for them to breastfeed their babies. If you want your baby to stay healthy then breastfeeding is the best solution because it provides complete nutrition that a baby needs for the first six months of life.

Breast milk is vital for the development of a child because it provides a baby with the necessary nutrients and helps the baby's immune system get stronger to fight virus and bacteria.

Wondering how this is related to your health? Did you know that breastfeeding can help reduce the size of the uterus and bring it back to the normal size after birth? Breastfeeding a baby lowers the risk of various problems including diabetes, leukemia, skin conditions and sudden infant death syndrome amongst others.

Women who breastfeed also stay healthy and are less likely to suffer from diabetes, ovarian cancer, breast cancer as well as postpartum depression. If this wasn't enough, breastfeeding also aids in weight loss and women who tend to breastfeed their babies for longer lose more weight in the long run and go back to their pre-pregnancy weight more comfortably.

Count Your Calories

I highly recommend you keep a tab on the kind of food you eat and make sure you know how many calories you are consuming. When it comes to calorie intake, a woman who breastfeeds needs to consume more calories in comparison to one who doesn't. Make sure you check with your doctor or dietitian to see how many calories you can consume. Nowadays you can download a variety of apps on your phone to keep track of your calories, and this helps you to choose a healthy lifestyle and cut down on larger meals to aid in healthy weight loss.

High Fiber Food

Post pregnancy your metabolism rates tend to drop a little which may add to the weight gain. Include high fiber in your meals since these foods not only help with digestion but also accelerate metabolism ensuring you lose weight faster. Fiber helps to keep your system clean and you also tend to eat smaller meals because fiber makes you feel fuller faster.

Choose to Eat Healthy Protein

Not only does protein make you stronger, but it also helps to keep you full and boosts your metabolism aiding in effective weight loss. Amongst healthy proteins, you should try to include as much of eggs and fish, dairy and lean meats in your diet as possible.

Stock Up on Healthy Snacks

The root cause of weight gain in eating unhealthy foods and you only way you will be able to eat this kind of food is when it's in your house. Each time you make a trip to the grocery store make sure you avoid buying unhealthy snacks and opt-in for healthy alternatives to munch on every time you feel hungry.

Avoid Processed Foods

Processed foods are very high and unhealthy fats along with sugar, calories, and salt. When you consume processed foods daily, your weight loss efforts will go in vain. Some of the fast foods you should avoid pre-packed cookies, chips, candies, ready mixes, and ready meals. Processed foods also contribute to eating disorders and can cause a lot of health complications for you. The best thing to do is to replace processed foods with nutrient-rich foods and start your weight loss journey on a healthy note.

Stop Consuming Alcohol

While alcohol in small quantities, such as red wine, does have certain health benefits, you need to make sure you stay away from alcohol if you want to lose weight. Alcohol is usually packed with a lot of calories and does not provide any kind of nutrition to your body.

Alcohol also causes a condition where the fat gets stored around the organs causing a belly fat. The worst part about alcohol is that it can cause a reduction in the volume of breast milk and very small amounts of alcohol can also be passed on to a baby through breast milk.

If you would like to drink regularly and you're breastfeeding a baby, you need to make sure you leave an enough gap between drinking and feeding your baby, so the alcohol is out of your body and not passed onto your baby. As a rule of thumb, you should wait at least 2 hours before you breastfeed your baby after drinking alcohol.

Exercising Helps

Exercising is not only helpful during your pregnancy, but it also helps to improve your health and lose weight after delivering a baby. There are various cardio exercises such as jogging, walking, interval training, cycling and running that will help you burn a lot of calories. These exercises also help to improve the health of your heart, and it reduces the risk of diabetes. However, you should know that just by exercising you will not be able to lose weight. '

You need to combine exercise with a good nutritional diet to help burn fat quickly. The combination of exercising and dieting is something you need to adapt to when looking to lose weight post-delivery. If you have had a C-section, you need to check with your doctor regarding the time to wait before you start exercising. You need to give your stomach and the pelvic area enough time to heal as rushing into exercising may cause health complications.

Resistance Training

Resistance training can help you lose weight and retain your muscle mass. When you combine resistance training along with a healthy diet, you will be able to lose weight effectively and improve your heart health. It goes without saying that you need approval from your doctor before you start weight training because your body has gone through a lot of stress and you may want to go easy a little bit. Another problem that comes with weight training is you will not find time to exercise when there is a baby that you must handle. You can try watching videos online or downloading mobile apps that will help you exercise while you are at home rather than heading out to a gym.

Drinking Water

Water is essential when it comes to staying healthy as well as losing weight. Staying hydrated is extremely important when you are breastfeeding your baby, and this is the reason you need to continue drinking water on a regular basis. Drinking enough water will also help reduce your calorie intake and it can reduce your appetite as well. Try to drink at least two liters of water daily as it can help with your weight loss and keep you hydrated. If you are exercising along with breastfeeding, then you may need to drink more water.

Get Sufficient Sleep

Sleep deprivation can affect your weight negatively. While getting sleep with a newborn child at home is extremely difficult, you should make sure that you sleep at every chance you get. You need to make sure that you are using the help of your partner as well as family members and friends so that you may be able to sleep while they take care of your baby.

Support Group

There are several support groups to help women with weight loss. When you join a support group, you will be able to stay motivated to achieve weight loss goals, and this will also ensure you get advice from other women who are on the same journey as you. Only women who have dealt with pregnancy will be able to understand the pain of another woman and this is where a support group comes in handy.

Asking Others for Help

You should never hesitate when it comes to asking your family members or friends for help. Several women usually go into depression because they do not have anyone around to help them and this can have a very negative impact on the baby as well. Your friends or family members can help with running errands or helping around the house. Some of them can even help take you to the doctor or your dietician, and this will go a long way in helping you with your weight loss process.

Avoid Consuming Sugar

Consuming sugar in the form of fruit juices or sugary drinks add a lot of calories and do not really provide nutrition to your body. You should also stay away from refined carbs so that you do not increase the risk of heart diseases and diabetes. Cutting down on added sugar will help you lose weight quickly, and it will also make your body healthier.

Chapter 14:
Newborn Must Haves

Pregnancy is tough and stressful, and your first pregnancy is usually going to be the most difficult because you don't really know what you should and shouldn't buy.

While it's essential for you to have a clear list of what's important, you should also understand unnecessary expenses and avoid them. I've discussed what needs to be avoided in the next chapter, and this one focuses on everything you need for your newborn baby. These are the kind of things you can add to your gift registry to cut down on your expenses and make sure you get the stuff you need.

Baby Diapers

You can never have enough diapers because babies need a lot of them and they go through at least five to seven changes a day and sometimes more, which means a pack of 50 diapers won't even last a week. There are some amazing baby infant diapers that you can invest in or add to your gift registry, so you are prepared when your baby poops. Make sure to select one that is designed for infant skin because an infant has very sensitive skin and using a diaper that is not designed for an infant could cause rash and infection.

Baby Wipes

Baby wipes are just as important as diapers because when you change your baby diapers you need something to clean up your baby and using cloth or cotton isn't recommended. If you are adding wipes to your gift registry, try registering for a bulk packet because these don't go bad for a long time and they will last you a couple of months. There are different kinds of baby wipes available so look for something that is soothing and designed for sensitive baby skin.

Diaper Rash Cream or Ointment

No matter how careful you are, your baby will end up with rashes on their bottom, and the best way to treat this rash or sore skin is to use a good quality baby rash cream or ointment. Always consult with your pediatrician to figure out which ointment or cream is good for your baby. You need to look for something that's not chemical based and has all organic natural materials, so it is safe on your baby's bottom.

Burp Cloth

It is highly recommended you invest in a ton of burp cloths because your baby is more likely to make a mess during the first three months and you should always be ready to clean up later. This cloth usually comes in a bundle of either 3 or 6 so add about two or three bundles to your gift registry just to keep some extra handy.

Feeding Bottles and Storage Bags

A lot of women need to get back to work soon after they have had a baby and, in such situations, you either need to pump milk out of the breast and store it in a bottle/bag or prepare formula for your baby. Irrespective of which route you take; you will need a lot of bottles and breast milk bags to store the milk. Try adding at least half a dozen bottles and bags to the list, so you have enough time to sterilize them before you use them.

Quick tip - Make sure you sterilize the bag and the bottle before you store milk in it because newborns are very sensitive, and the stomach cannot handle anything out of the ordinary.

Rubbing Alcohol and Cotton Swabs

Once you bring your baby back home from the hospital, you need to clean the umbilical cord. For you to do this, you must use rubbing alcohol and cotton swabs. This is something not a lot of people will tell you about, and most mothers are not even prepared about what needs to be done for them to clean the umbilical cord regularly. Make sure to ask a midwife or the doctor to teach you the correct method of cleaning the cord, so you don't hurt your baby.

First Aid Kit

A first aid kit should be at the top of your priority list even before your baby is born. I didn't realize this until later when my husband panicked and ran out the door to the nearest pharmacy to get one. Your first aid kit should have a nose sucker, thermometer and basic medications your doctor has recommended for your baby.

Nail Clippers

While we're about a first aid kit, I'd like to talk about the importance of nail clippers specifically designed for infants. Cutting the nails of a baby is so underrated, and parents usually believe they can use any nail clippers, but this is not the case. I didn't realize the importance of a nail clipper until I had scratch marks all over my breasts because it's my baby's long nails and my inability to cut them with an adult nail clipper. There are safe to use baby nail clippers available that you can safely cut your baby's nails with. I highly recommend getting one of these.

Baby Formula

If you plan on getting back to work in a few weeks post-delivery, you need to consider getting your baby used to the formula because you will not manage to pump out a lot of milk and store it in order to feed your baby throughout the day. While breastmilk is ideally recommended for the first six months, if you can't give your baby breastmilk you can always alternate between formula and breastmilk depending on how hectic your schedule is.

Pacifiers

Most babies need a pacifier to keep them calm and help them feel secure when they're not breastfeeding. If you plan on getting your baby a pacifier, look for soft pacifiers that won't hurt your babies' gums. Try investing in a couple of them so that you can keep sterilizing and cleaning them from time to time.

Breast Pump

I can't stress enough on how effective this pump was when I got back to work. While it is a personal choice, you can always try getting on manual one that doesn't cost so much and see whether it works well for you or not. The benefit of using a breast pump is that your baby is not dependent on you and you have a little freedom and time where you could just go relax and rejuvenate yourself.

Baby Lotion

Baby lotion is essential to ensure that the baby does not suffer from dry skin or any kind of rashes after having a bath. It is essential to make sure that your baby is comfortable once he or she has had a bath and al lotion will help soothe the skin from outside and keep it moist from within.

Wash Cloths

You need to have a few washcloths in hand when you have a baby around. It is important to know that your baby will drool most of the time and there will be a lot of wiping that you will need to do around the mouth and the chest area. It is best not using a towel because a towel may cause irritation to the baby's skin and this is where a washcloth will come very handy.

Baby Shampoo

You need to take care of your baby's hair from the first month itself. Apart from investing and lotions you also need to make sure you invest in the best baby shampoo that will help treat your baby's hair with care. There are several no-tear baby shampoo brands you can consider. You won't need to purchase a very big bottle because you need to use a very tiny drop each time you bathe your baby.

Baby Bathtub

Many people use the adult bathtub to bathe their baby. It is important you purchase a baby bathtub, so your baby has his or her own space when they are having a bath. A baby bathtub is not slippery, and it is safe for babies to use. Adult bathtubs, on the other hand, can be slippery and if your baby has the habit of standing up while having a bath, this could cause accidents and unwanted injuries which could be avoided with the baby bathtub.

Crib Along with Mattress

Getting a crib for your baby is essential and you can also ensure that you get a crib that will match the decor of the baby room. While purchasing a crib, you also need to make sure you invest in a top-quality mattress that will keep your baby very comfortable. The reason you need to purchase a baby mattress is because you would not want a baby to sleep on anything that could irritate his or her skin.

Bed Linens

Newborns are extremely messy when it comes to pooping or even throwing up after eating. While it is not advisable to feed a baby in the crib, if you must do that, you need to make sure you invest in a good set of bed linens. It is always good to invest in three or four sets of linens so that you can keep swapping them as and when the baby dirties one of them.

Blankets

Swaddling a newborn baby is essential, and therefore you need to purchase blankets that will help the baby feel extremely secure and warm. Newborn babies need to be wrapped tightly because they are used to being snug in the womb. This is where a swaddling blanket comes extremely handy. If your baby is not very comfortable with being swaddled, then you can leave one hand outside the blanket, and the baby will think that he or she is not wrapped.

Clothes for Your Baby

You need to invest in a lot of onesies and gowns that will make it easy for you to change the diaper for your baby. Most of the clothes for babies these days are available with the button at the bottom that will allow you to change the diaper very easily without having to take out the top. Clothes are available in various sizes but always make sure that you invest in something that would fit a 3-month-old because your baby would grow very fast, and there is no point purchasing new clothes every month.

Socks
A newborn needs socks all the time. Although one may feel that they do not really need to cover their baby's feet in summer, it is important because your baby's skin is very sensitive, and you would not want to expose the skin to the elements. This is the reason you also need to purchase a hat that will come handy during the summer as well as the winter.

Car Seat
A car seat is the most important item that you need to purchase for your baby. You should always purchase a new car seat as opposed to purchasing a used car seat because the used car seat may not be able to withstand a crash. The installation of the car seat must be done properly. Look for a car seat that has excellent safety ratings.

Stroller
It is important to have a stroller; however, you can always combine a stroller along with the car seat that you purchase. There are several brands that offer this combination; however, you need to check the safety aspect of the seat before you go ahead and get excited about the combo offer.

Diaper Bags

This is something that you will have to purchase irrespective of how old your baby is. When you move around with your baby outside the house, you will want to carry extra diapers along with creams as well as baby wipes. Always look for a diaper bag that has an insulated section that will help keep bottles cold or warm as per your food requirements.

Chapter 15:
Don't Fall for These Money Traps

Every parent wants to give their baby the best, and there's nothing wrong with this. However, you need to learn to draw a line between what's necessary for your baby and what is an unnecessary expense. There are going to be a lot of new parents who will come and advise you with regards to baby products that they believe are must-haves. Here are a few of these things I believe are a complete waste of money and should be avoided.

Baby Wipe Warmer

I never really understood the concept of a baby wipe warmer because you don't have to wipe your baby's bottom with a warm wipe since cold ones are always preferred. Warm wipes could cause a little irritation on your baby's skin, and unless you are storing your wipes in the freezer, you won't need this warmer. If it is cold in the city you live in, just warm a little water and dip the wipe inside the water before using it on your baby. It's economical and makes a lot of sense.

Baby Seat

A baby seat is something you need to avoid, and while it has become a popular item to have in a household, it is best avoided. It is dangerous forcing your baby to sit even before they are ready to walk, and this could cause a major accident. When your baby becomes ready to sit just use a normal chair!

Talcum Powder
Baby talcum powder has been popular, and people are so used to patting the baby's bottoms with this powder every time they have a bath. However, this is best avoided because there have been reports of baby talcum powder being linked to ovarian cancer.

Baby Food Blender
A baby blender works just as effectively as your blender, and it does nothing different. You can blend your baby's food in your regular blender and investing in a baby blender makes no sense.

Expensive Swings and Rockers
Most new parents get frustrated when their baby does not sleep because they need to be held all the time. One of the things that most parents do is invest in expenses swings or rockers that they feel will put the baby to sleep. What these parents don't realize is the child will eventually start sleeping on their own, and the rocker will just be a waste of money lying in the corner of the room. As parents, you should take turns to hold the baby because this phase is not going to last long, and babies outgrow it very quickly.

Emergency Bottle and Formula

When you are not breastfeeding, it is always advisable to purchase formula because it will help provide nourishment to the baby. However, if you are breastfeeding and you do not have to feed anything else to the baby there is no point in purchasing formula just for the heck of it. Having formula around could even be a barrier to you breastfeeding your baby and this is the reason you need to keep it away for as long as possible when you are breastfeeding your baby.

Baby Shoes

These are a complete no-no. Your baby is not going to walk until he or she is about 7 to 8 months old. There is no point in purchasing shoes for a 1 month or 2-month-old baby because it is never going to be used. There are parents who spend hundreds of dollars on expensive branded shoes just because they want their baby to look good. Making such investments is of no use until your baby starts walking.

Baby Walkers

Let me make one thing straight - a walker will not teach your baby to walk. Most babies can figure out walking on their own. We should all remember that our parents learned to work even when walkers were not even invented. Some babies learn to work later than other babies; however, this should not be a cause for concern. Forcing your baby to walk with the assistance of a walker is not recommended.

Hooded Towels

Babies need towels however; they do not need towels that come with a hood. Babies grow at a very fast pace in the first year and purchasing a towel with the tiny little hood will be of no use in a couple of weeks.

Pregnancy is a long and beautiful journey that has its ups and downs. While you can try to figure out a few hacks to help you through your journey, you also need to remind yourself that every individual is different and what works well for someone else may not work as effectively for you. Take time to figure out your rhythm, and you'll get better with each day.

The journey of parenting begins from conception, and it's a role you need to live up to, every day of your life. While you'll enjoy it for the most part, for the times you don't - just take a deep breath and start over! It's not about perfection, but about enjoying parenthood and making the most of it.

If you find this book helpful in anyway a review to support my endeavors is much appreciated.

Mindful Pregnancy for New Moms

Catherine Taylor

www.ingramcontent.com/pod-product-compliance
Lightning Source LLC
Chambersburg PA
CBHW060451080526
44584CB00015B/1404